AF593428

THE IDEAL LEADERSHIP HANDBOOK

(For The Twenty First Century Corporate World & The Church Of God)

Rev. (Dr.) Victor Mbah

The Ideal Leadership Handbook
First edition – September 2022
Author: Dr. Victor Mbah

Contact: Dr. Victor Mbah.
Email: omegahouston@yahoo.com
Phone: 832-887-7105

Inspiration: Holy Spirit

All rights reserved under international copyright law. Written permission must be secured from the publisher to use or reproduce any part of this book, except for brief quotations in critical reviews or articles.

Copyright ©2022 OGM

Printed in the United States of America

Unless otherwise stated, all Scripture quotations are taken from the King James Version of The Holy Bible, Complete Jewish Bible and Amplified Version

TABLE OF CONTENTS

Chapter 1
UNDERSTANDING CHURCH LEADERSHIP AND THE LEADER...7

1. What Is Leadership...7
2. What Leadership Is Not. 8
3. Who Is A Leader? 9

Chapter 2
CHURCH LEADERSHIP PERSPECTIVES DRAWN FROM WATERFALL METHODOLOGY..19

4. Waterfall Leadership Methodology (Old Testament Law of Moses Methodology) 19
5. Critical approach to what is generally known as the advantages of waterfall methodology 23
6. Shortcomings of Waterfall methodology 26

Chapter 3
CHURCH LEADERSHIP PERSPECTIVES DRAWN FROM AGILE LEADERSHIP APPROACH..............................35

7. What is Agile Leadership APPROACH (a Bottom-Up Management Approach)? 35
8. What is Agile Servant Leadership... 36
9. Who Is An Agile Servant Leader. 38
10. Agile/Grace Servant Leadership in the body of Christ. ...39

Chapter 4
STRENGTHS AND WEAKNESSES OF AGILE SERVANT LEADERSHIP...49

11. Strengths of Agile Servant Leadership/Grace Leadership Method. 49
12. Weaknesses of a Bottom-Up Management Approach 56

Chapter 5
HOW TO TRANSFORM CHURCH LEADERSHIP FROM WATERFALL TO AGILE SYSTEM 59

13. Introduction. 59
14. Steps to Implement Agile Transformation through
Servant Leadership 62
15. Implementation Process 65
16. Strategies of Handling Opponents to the Work. 68
17. Agile Approach Ceremonies And Their Relevance
To The Church. 71
18. The Twelve Agile Manifesto Principles. 83
19. The Four Values of The Agile Manifesto. 89
20. The Five Scrum Values 93

Chapter 6
UNDERSTANDING THE MOTIVATING POWERS OF A SERVANT- LEADER 103

Chapter 7
THE CHALLENGES OF GRACE LEADERSHIP METHOD AND HOW TO CURB THEM 115

21. The Challenge when you are not a principal leader. 115
22. The Challenge when you are the principal Leader. 121
23. The Challenge of Transitioning Leadership 134

Chapter 8
THE NEW TESTAMENT WAY OF SELECTING AND PROMOTING A LEADER TO THE NEXT LEVEL. .... .139

24. Things to Consider while choosing or promoting a
Leader to a top position.. 139

Chapter 9
DESTROYING THE SACRED COWS OF LEADERSHIP. 145

Chapter 10
QUICK TEST OF EFFECTIVE SERVANT LEADERSHIP. 155

Decision Page..157

ACKNOWLEDGMENTS

With deep appreciation, I acknowledge the support and guidance of the following people who helped make this book possible:

Thanks to **Juliana King University** for the courses that have helped shape my growth in Leadership and Management. Special thanks go to my wife, Lady Muriel Mbah, my backbone and collaborator in ministry work. She has served as a sounding board for ideas and has earned my undying appreciation and respect. Thanks to Manto Sandio Mirabelle, She put in countless hours in typing, retyping, and helping me in proofreading all of the material that has made this book possible, her organization and techniques, and anecdotes were no small job, but she made it look easy. Hearty thanks also go to our entire church **Omega Gospel Ministries,** their support cannot be overemphasized. Hats off to the church leadership throughout this process, for the superb contributions in shaping this manuscript. Lady Muriel and I both thank them for their enthusiastic support of leadership.

A leader is the person who convinces other people to follow by his or her example. A leader inspires confidence in other people and moves them to action by doing same.

CHAPTER ONE

UNDERSTANDING CHURCH LEADERSHIP AND THE LEADER

What is Leadership?

From my extensive study and experience in leadership, I observed that multiple definitions of leadership exist, although the different definitions generally converge in the theory that great leaders have the ability to make strategic and visionary decisions and convince others to follow those decisions. The consensus is leaders create a vision and can successfully get others to work toward achieving it. They do this by setting direction and getting people excited and motivated to work toward the vision and achieve the result.

Many in-depth definitions of leadership have emerged but we are going to study that of Kevin Kruse, founder and CEO of a leadership habits app that turns millennial managers into legacy leaders' defined leadership as being a *"process of social influence, which maximizes the efforts of others, towards the achievement of a goal"*

The key elements of Kelvin Kruse definition are:

Leadership stemming from social influence and not authority, power or dominance

Leadership requiring others and that implies they don't need to be "direct reports" You will observe there is no mention of personality traits, attributes, or even a title; there are many styles, many paths, to effective leadership.

It as well includes a goal and not influence without any intended result

Lastly, what makes this definition outstanding and separate from many academic definitions out there is the inclusion of "maximizes the efforts".

Although the terms leadership and management are sometimes used interchangeably, they are not the same concept. Leadership and management are not synonymous. Thought, there is aspect of management in leader-ship, leadership isn't management. Leaders overseas but managers administer.

What Leadership is Not

For the sake of where we are heading to, as you proceed through this treasure you are holding bear in mind the following understanding of what leadership is not;

Leadership has nothing to do with seniority or one's position in the hierarchy of an organization. Most people talk about leadership referring to the senior most executives in the organization. They are just that, senior executives. Leadership doesn't automatically happen when you reach a certain pay role. Hopefully, you might find it there, but there are no guarantees anyway. This is because; leadership has nothing to do with titles. Just because you have a C-level title, doesn't automatically make you a "*leader.*" You don't need a title to lead. In fact, you can be a leader in your church assembly, your neighborhood, in your family, all without having a title.

Also, understand that leadership has nothing to do with personal attributes. When vocalize the word "leader" most people think of a domineering, taking-charge charismatic or autocratic individual, forgetting the word "*leadership*" isn't an adjective. We don't need extroverted charismatic traits to practice leadership and those with charisma don't automatically lead.

Leadership is not power and control but about social skill.

Who is a Leader?

When your mind pictures great leaders, who come to you?

Some see impactful figures like Our Lord Jesus Christ, Moses, Gideon, Deborah, David, Nehemiah, Apostle

Paul, etc. when it comes to the secular world some see Mahatma Gandhi and Martin Luther King Jr., or perhaps Nelson Mandela and Winston Churchill might also come to mind. However, consider this rhetorical question, was it simply their position that made them good leaders, or was it something beyond?

Reasonable explorations of the question, "who is a leader?" include:

A leader is someone who inspires passion and motivation in followers. The leader empowers the team members to embrace their own unique leadership qualities and act with independently.

A leader is someone with a vision and the path to realizing it.

A leader is someone who ensures their team has support and tools to achieve their goals.

A leader is the person who convinces other people to follow by his or her example. A leader inspires confidence in other people and moves them to action by doing same.

A leader may be any of those things, but a good leader possesses all the above characteristics.

However, leaders tend to exhibit seven major components which produces effective leadership: self-confidence, purpose, motivation, strong communication and management skills, creative and innovative thinking, empathy, perseverance in the face of failure, willingness to take risks, team vision and openness to change which let to continual improvement, level headedness and is reactive in times of crisis.

Sequel to the above, my question is *"Are you a leader? Can you become a leader?* The answer is yes! In this, I will be showing you certain signs that reveal the leader within youn***g the Bible, we see Apostle Paul writing to Timothy and telling him to look for people with leadership qualities.***

"...If a man desire the office... 1 Timothy 3:1". That connotes a desire. It is thrilling to note that Apostle Paul wanted people who had the desire for ministerial office and Timothy was instructed to look for certain qualities in those who had the desire for it. I therefore stress that, a desire to lead is a sign of a leader within you.

- ✓ If you constantly have the urge to help people out of their predicament, it is a great sign that God has given you the gift of leadership. You are full of compassion and desire to serve others with the good things you have, is a great sign of leadership. Apostle Paul was constantly burdened by the desire to help the Jews

- ✓ "***Brethren, my heart's desire and prayer to God for Israel is, that they might be saved. Romans 10:1"*** All true leadership stems from the burden to help people whom you love.

- ✓ The major sign of leadership is the burden and desire which compels the leader into action. That over-whelming burden/compassion/desire is the common feature in every potential leader. Daniel had the burden for the Jews in Jerusalem after discovering the prophesy of Jeremiah about the seventy years of Captivity, he understood that the seventy years was over and they were entering seventy one years, this catalyzed Daniel's calling. Also, look at the plea of Apostle Paul, ***"I say the truth in Christ, I lie not, my conscience also bearing me witness in the Holy Ghost, That I have great heaviness and continual sorrow in my heart. For I could wish that myself were accursed from Christ for my brethren, my kinsmen according to the flesh: Romans 9:1-3***

- ✓ In the same vein, some people greatest hurt become their potential domain of leadership. After going through difficulties in life and recovering from their pain, they have a strong desire and burden to help others avoid the pain and suffering they went through. Faithful parent would want their children to avoid the same mistake they made and be better than them. ***Jesus said, Verily, verily, I say unto you, He that believeth on me, the works that I do shall he do also; and greater works than these shall he do John 14: 12***

> As a true leader, Jesus Christ wanted his followers to be better than himself.

Conversely, this doesn't rebuff the fact that, there are some people who have a desire for money, power and fame. Not knowing, they have an ulterior motive and their intention is to manipulate others and use the position of leadership for self-aggrandizement like some of the political leaders in the world today. That is not leadership! It is witchcraft. A typical example of such leaders is Demas who deserted Apostle Paul and moved from one church to the other for self gain:

2 Timothy 4:10 "For Demas has forsaken me, having loved this present world, and is departed unto Thessalonica; Crescens to Galatia, Titus unto Dalmatia"

Abimelech the son of Jerubbaal (Gideon) that he had with his concubine in Shekem, the whole of ***Judges Chapter nine*** proves he is someone who preyed ruthlessly on his people and the end of it was the death of the seventy sons of Gideon.

The disciples of Jesus cajoled for power, fighting who was going to be the greatest. Jesus warned them that leadership entailed a lot of responsibility and suffering. Many of the disciples of Jesus tasted the suffering and hardship the leader suffers, as many of them were killed and tortured. Jesus warned them who would desire to be great must be a servant of the people. Unfortunately, some churches have also had leaders, who like vampires, have sucked away the wealth and the life of the church and frustrated many souls. It is crystal clear that leaders with wrong motives were common in Peter's time and they are certainly common in our time. Peter warned against this in his letter to the church. ***"The elders which are among you I exhort, who am also an elder, and a witness of the sufferings of Christ, and also a partaker of the glory that shall be revealed: Feed the flock of God which is among you, taking the oversight thereof, not by constraint, but willingly; not for filthy illegal gain, but of a ready mind; Neither as being lords over God's heritage, but being ensamples to the flock" 1 Peter 5:1-3.***

Leadership crises are a global trend causing global poverty, inhuman treatment, financial and economic unrest, wars, immigration and refugee crises. In an age when leadership is viewed as a place of enrichment, arrogance, and financial interest, not realizing it is a great challenge; ineffective, unwise, corrupt and greedy leadership will only sink and destroy the church, as well as the nation. God is looking out for men and women that have stood the test of time and are willing to agree to take up the mantle of leadership and pay the price thereof.

In a time like this, a time of global crisis and turbulence, confusion, racial tension, chaos, hate, division, healthcare crises, wars ravaging the world, refugee crises threatening the world, a threat of World

War Nuclear looming, etc. Unless we have godly, wise, compassionate and principled leadership, the world will degenerate into chaos. We need trans-formational leaders with exceptional leadership qualities who will attend to the followers' needs, values, and morals.

Typically, the Biblical character, Nehemiah epitomized the transformational leader. Nehemiah was a Jewish biblical figure who appeared in the historical events in Israel during the Jewish exile in Babylon. It was a time of extreme hardship, shame, and ridicule for the Jewish people just as we see the world today: their homes were plundered and they were carried away by the Babylonians; and scattered all over the world because of disobedience to God's will.

Nehemiah was a godly man who feared God, distinguished, efficient, noble, and the king loved him, he served as a cup bearer at the king's palace in Persia but cared deeply for the concerns of the people; his entire vision was driven upon hearing of the distress of the people of Jerusalem and Judah. Coupled with the Nehemiah purpose of setting out to rebuild the walls so "proper worship of God" could be restored, was also the urgent need to rescue the poor from oppression and slavery. He did not hoard material goods for himself; rather, he gave himself for the people, he refused to receive his lawful allowance from the people while as governor and caring for their moral and spiritual needs by addressing the issue of intermarriage.

Nehemiah boldly confronts Jewish oppression of the poor. When he arrived, the people cried out because they were oppressed by the nobles and rulers. Their lands were taken, houses and vine yards so they can't even buy food to eat. Families were on siege and in great suffering as they couldn't feed their children. These were Jewish leaders. Nehemiah was angry and scolded the rulers, nobles and rebuked them. He told them it was not right and they should restore the vine yards and the houses back to the people, and they listened to him. They responded "*We will restore them and we will require nothing of them." Nehemiah 5: 1-12*

Additionally, He did not deviate from what God called him to do, or his vision and destiny to pursue other irrelevant material things that have destroyed some leaders like the love for money and power, women, or sex, etc. He was completely focused on the burden of his struggling people and that is what the leader should be concerned with. A leader shouldn't take advantage of the weak but be concerned with the problems of the people who elected him or her to serve; whether in politics, corporations, or churches, or any leadership position. Nehemiah finished the work of rebuilding the wall and the city.

That desire within you to help others is the sign of a call of God upon your life and it is time to help. God wants to raise you up to do just that as you read this book, may the anointing to lead in your God gifted area be upon you in the name of Jesus! Same for everyone reading this book, I acknowledge that this is for the betterment of the body of Christ, and I pray the Father that this revelation taken out of my Spirit, be imputed in the spirit of His people that He have chosen like He did for Moses and the seventy elders to lighten the work in Jesus Name.

Considering every one of you as potential leaders, you shouldn't be deprived of this knowledge. As you go through this book I desire that, whether you are already a performing leader or futuristic, you will benefit from it and it will help you in all sphere of influence. As the Holy Spirit leads us, it will bring a lasting transformation and unity in the workforce more than ever before. Some of you that are yet to step into the full potentials of their leadership capacity and have always felt like ministry is for a particular set of people will now understand that it is for all, therefore, "***it is our thing and not their thing***" as they would fondly say. Some of you that have been warming the pews, thinking you are not worthy or you are not part of it will now understand there is a paradigm reversal. It is good to appreciate the choir when they sing, it is good to appreciate any other department when they minister or function but how you are participating to make the work better is most significant. So this teaching will create in you a sense of awareness that everyone is useful. It will create an avenue for the leadership qualities in you to be exposed and harness for you to serve and be blessed in the house of God including all domain of life you find yourself.

Proverbs 16:18

"Pride goes before destruction,
and an haughty spirit before a fall",

Chapter Two

================

CHURCH LEADERSHIP PERSPECTIVES DRAWN FROM WATERFALL METHODOLOGY

Waterfall Leadership Methodology (Old Testament Law of Moses Methodology)

Waterfall also called the Top - bottom method of overseeing businesses which is commonly known as a traditional method and also referred to as autocratic leadership, is a management process driven by a business' upper level of executives. Senior Leaders create company-wide decisions that trickle down to lower departments. The decisions are first weighed on variables like frequency and severity, and then made based on the higher or lower levels of such variables. Upper management gathers and acts upon the knowledge, which employees carry out, they are superimposed on members whether they like it or not, they are obliged to adhere to them. Meaning, management dictates to teams exactly what to do. Deciding power resides with team leadership, instead of being distributed amongst team members. The top-down policy is widely practiced in corporate America and around the world.

However, recently the Top-bottom leadership style has not been that effective. It has its loopholes which have been greatly challenged and companies are now transiting to what is known as the Agile leadership style which inculcates in the minds of every participant a sense of control, thus giving everyone from the bottom to the top the opportunity to lead or effect changes. In this leadership, everyone counts; you are employed because your CV portrays the attributes of the job's suitability. So when it comes to decision making, it is not just going to be impose on you but they will collaborate with you for effective management.

Am going to relate these methodologies spiritually, and this is going to revolutionize the Church if properly imbibe, this is divine as it was given to me by revelation. As the time of writing this book, I was doing my PhD in theology and some of the courses that we did there like leadership and management, makes me to see things from different angles, you can't study and remain the same, reason managerial positions in companies are paid differently because they do most of the thinking and implementation.

Looking at it from the spiritual angle, it is imperative to say that, leadership was done in the Old Testament, in that same pattern. Obviously the world borrowed that from the bible which was the era of the Law of Moses whereby if one doesn't obey the law, such a person faces the consequences and there are no negotiations. Any transgression of the law leads to severe punishment or even death. A case in point is when the woman caught in adultery was brought to Jesus quoting the law of Moses as they were about to stone her to death.

The shortcomings of Waterfall Leadership Method and Its Execution

Execution of Waterfall methodology

The main problem with waterfall is the execution, top management is the one who thinks on how best the Company can be in the future. Am not in any way downgrading positional leadership, am talking about implementation of what have been instill in them, how do you implement this to affect everyone? Example we have five elders in the church and if we are looking only upon those five elders to do everything, then we have failed as a church. At the end of each year, we have a leadership meeting followed by members' appraisal where everyone brings in his or her opinion; we identify our flaws and work on how we can improve on them. In the corporate world it is called retrospective. We go into the annual, bi-annual work and make amendments. I came to understand that we were practicing agile to an extent but this time, we brought it to every department of the Church. We understood that our women and men should be able to meet and draft recommendations for the betterment of the department. Most importantly note that the reason is to get reliable contributions from every member. So the period which some members were neglected is over and the time have come that everyone must be valued.

Waterfall system simply tells us about the law way things were done, in *Exodus 20:1-10 you see the many thou shalt not.* Moses gives ordinances on what should be done and it will remain in that setting, if we have to abide by such law, we will never make heaven because we transgress the law every day, with this, it is obvious that waterfall is already failing because we most time do the contrary of what the bible says, thus falling short of the Glory. It is in this view that when God saw that the law could not work, He decided to establish a new system in ***Luke 22:24-29.*** We see how the law is top bottom, it says any of you that want to be the leader, should first of all be a servant. In the corporate world, waterfall methodology says leadership is a position but in the agile system, leadership is performance.

Critical approach to what is generally known as the advantages of waterfall methodology:

1. Those who buy this method think that operating in such leadership style there is a decreased risk involved in the decision-making process when lower level employees are taken out of the equation, since the highest level of management is usually the most informed and most knowledgeable about the work/business, it reduce the risk of failure. They believe in themselves not God as compared to the church, the church believed that there is a firm assurance of not failing if it maintains a certain number of Pastors, elders, leaders. That if we maintain the status quo, there is no risk or fear of failure.

   Ironically, it might seem right but it is not so because since the top level management is usually the one that inform the lower level of what they should do, there is always the need that they want collaboration. If the top will tell the bottom level people what to do, that is not in line with what management is saying, even though they feel at the top, the risk factor is eliminated, but those at the bottom are crying out loud that, they are not collaborating and simply just working under compulsion.

   Proverbs 16:18 "Pride goes before destruction, and an haughty spirit before a fall", meaning top level management is confident that because they have a leadership team that they master for years and they are proficient and so they don't need any change in the leadership. This proves that God has no place in that church or company; they have seen their capacity and turn to trust in the arm of men. My question is, *what of those you are yet to exploit and see their capacity as well? Where have you kept them?* how do you know whether God does not have an added value in them for the advancement of the ministry? How would you know if God have something different he wants to instill in the church through some body that you have never experienced the manifestation of their gift.

2. They also think it gives strong management skills. The upper authorities in a company will be able to determine best practices and reach goals easier with decisions created and enforced at the highest ranks of a business. This is because of familiarity within themselves, for example, you already know a particular pastor, deacon or HOD so well and feel you don't need any other etc. We are good at that; we have every ground for complacency. This is a wrong mindset, *why?* From the Agile or Grace perspective, this prove that God is taken off the management and their trust is instead turned to men and it cycles like that when one leaves, there is a huge vacuum. In the kingdom agile system, God comes first, he is the one we put

our trust in believing that he can empower anyone for effective work.

3. Traditional leadership strives to achieve success by tweaking workflow and metrics rather than by empowering individuals. To them, it helps minimize the cost and maximize potential. Lower level employees are free to complete their own tasks unique to their role in the company and aren't saddled with the responsibility of setting company-wide goals. They prefer to keep the ones they already have because they are not ready to undergo the stress and the cost of training others. The rhetorical question to consider is what if of a sudden these people are no more? The Bible says in ***Haggai 1:5-7 "Now therefore thus says the LORD of hosts; consider your ways. All of you have sown much, and bring in little; all of you eat, but all of you have not enough; all of you drink, but all of you are not filled with drink; all of you clothe you, but there is none warm; and he that earns wages earns wages to put it into a bag with holes. Thus says the LORD of hosts; consider your ways."*** Those in the world might do it in order to pilfer or for some selfish interest best known to them. In the church, not as if we don't have the means to run the cost but the main issue is a lack of trust. Even though we feel like cutting down the cost, we are never satisfied with the money we make, we

saved and it is not still sufficient. So this is not a cogent reason for imploring this method. It doesn't add up and because of these, creativity is limited ***Psalms 78:41 "Yea, they turned back and tempted God, and limited the Holy One of Israel."***

They limited the Almighty God by trusting only a few; they thought to be the best. I love what one of our lecturers at Bible College in South Africa Pastor Cornell, told us when we were doing our live practical he said "*if I can't be humble enough to sit and hear you preach, then am not worthy to be your teacher.*" Invariably it will be pride for him not to sit for the 15mins of live practical and listen to those he have trained, then he is what is he teaching them?

Shortcomings of Waterfall methodology

1. **Top-down management limit Creativity:**

   Employees are unable to contribute to the overall goals of the company. They ignore the skills, talents, and experiences that bottom-level employees/workers have, which can lead to suboptimal decision-making. Some end up frustrated and lack motivation to perform. It creates a barrier and limits the Almighty God from expressively using those submitted under such system.

2. **The Boss has the final word:**

   Should you need to make immediate changes; a top-down change (also known as an executive-driven change) can come into play to resolve any problems within an organization, bypassing a slower decision making process involving lower level employees. If the boss doesn't have a clear idea of what the project involves, but still has the final word, then the whole project could fail. But they have come to conclude that only those at top knows better and so only them can lead since the system is used to them. These are the convincing evidence of those that operate in the system. ***1 Corinthians 4:7 "For who makes you to differ from another? and what have you that you did not receive? now if you did receive it, why do you glory, as if you had not received it?"*** Every talent you have is gifted, so you cannot limit yourself on the one or few people you know they are talented. We are saying in essence that this method of leadership is faulty and not fit for the New Testament Church because God can bless and endow others with many gifts for more effective work than the person you substantiate the most.

3. **Moreover, It is a Dictatorial/ Oppressive system of leadership**:

   Ezekiel 22:29, *"The people of the land have used oppression, and exercised robbery, and*

have vexed the poor and needy: yea, they have oppressed the stranger wrongfully". Their approach seems oppressive to the employees or workers as their words are Supreme. They are oppressive dictators and I apologetically say this is exactly how some of our African pastors operate.

4. **This method brings distraction and oppression in the way of operation.**

   A leader is seen like a god and his words become the absolute. It is likened to a dictatorial oppressive regime of the vampire political and religious leaders we see everywhere. Have you been to a church where lives are controlled, they literally dictates people life, even a couple that are about to get married have no say in matters concerning themselves, they dictate to you the type of wedding gown, venue etc. This is bondage.

   While Agile will get to know why things are done the way it is being done. Once you don't operate in a way that you can dialogue, you become a dictator leader, since no one can bring in his/her opinion.

5. **Another disadvantage of waterfall method is that it slows down response to challenges.**

   It can take time for upper management to establish a solution because they might not have full knowledge of the issue on ground and are limited minds in contributing to decisions. when a challenge arises as a result of a decision making, it might take longer time for the top management to come out with solution because, they are not privy to the basics, the lower level staff are aware of things they might be limited to and this becomes difficult for them to bring effective and lasting solutions. Also, some workers don't make themselves available outside of business hours; even if there is a contingency within their capacity to handle. It is frustrating for a leader having someone refuse to do a task because it is "*not his/her job.*"

He is concern about his role while agile is concerned about his goal Leader's goal is to get the job done, to fulfill the vision of the organization and its leader. That often means doing whatever it takes. The bottom often doesn't have any option than to wait for the top to get it done themselves. Such system does not work again in corporate America. The Church also has to shift from it ***Revelation 3:15 "I know your works, that you are neither cold nor hot: I would you were cold or hot".*** We can't be in-between, we can't move the way God is leading us if we are neither hot nor cold.

6. **The system makes the people feel like strangers with no sense of belonging:**

They feel sidelined and have no sense of belonging. What the principal leader says is final, and the bottom level staff has no say. Tasks are determined and filtered down company's lines without any confusion because business goals are set by upper management and will not be affected by outside opinions. The people know they are part of the company but don't get involve fully because they are limited to the scope of what they have to do.

Conversely in Agile or Grace Leadership approach, ***Ephesians 2:19 says "Now therefore all of you are no more strangers and foreigners, but fellow citizens with the saints, and of the household of God"*** You can't remain a stranger in a church were you have been more than 6 years. Generally, only three months' probation period is given in companies and when you onboard, you have two to three weeks induction period even though it differs with some companies. How then will someone sit in the church for more than six months, still feels like a stranger without getting involved? That mentality is buried today in the name of Jesus Christ. We are members of the same household, we are one and we are in it together.

7. Waterfall methodology promotes individualism and competition. Everyone wants to be the best above others, they work to impress their boss what I call "*eye service.*" Selfishness creeps in and shut up every means of effective collaboration

with each other in the work place because all they seek is self-glory; this should be avoided in the body of Christ.

In waterfall methodology workers compete with each other but in Agile methodology workers complete each other's. The agile system foster team spirit, they all succeed or fail as a team. It doesn't matter whom you're helping, whether it's your boss, a peer, or someone working for you because when you help someone in the team, you help the whole team. ***Philippians 2:3 "Let nothing be done through strife or vainglory; but in lowliness of mind let each esteem other better than themselves."***

Team success is achieved independently of the leadership qualities of an individual because teams that share a vision conveyed by leadership are more motivated and deliver more and better output than if they simply follow orders from superiors. Grace Leadership approach emphasis that it becomes "*we*" and not "*I*" and replace the term "*individuals*" with "*people*" because being agile means being team-oriented.

I do invite men of God in our church for programs, after their introduction, they in turn say something good about me. In the real perspective, inviting them appears we esteem them better than ourselves but none of them have ever sat down without putting **Philippians 2:3** into practice. It is a norm in the pastoral cycle, they are careful enough to acknowledge the other. No matter how much you feel more anointed than your hosts you must acknowledge them, just the fact that he shared their platform with you is an honor. That is why when we esteem them, they do same in return. That neither reduces us nor exchanges the greatness of our anointing; it is simply, a display of love in the brotherhood, a form of appreciating each other gifting, a balance is maintained and we don't jealous one another.

8. Waterfall doesn't promote an environment where people are encouraged and motivated. The waterfall, law system breath pretense, one wants to always show that he or she is the best. Your best is not about what you do but about "we" as a team do. When **OGM** succeed, it is not about Pastor Victor but about us all, so don't deceive yourself by placing the success of **OGM** on one particular individual. **OMG** is us; it portrays our oneness, our togetherness, our unity and love. Bring this understanding to your department, your business, firm etc., and don't compete with one another, instead you encourage each other and make each other better because everyone is unique in his/her ways of delivery.

Waterfall is selfish while agile is selfless, the fact that we come from different backgrounds and God brought us here as a Church, mean we need to complement, motivate, encourage, uplift each other and not to of bring them down. ***Ecclesiastical 4:9 "Two are better than one; because they have a good reward for their labour." Proverbs 27:17"Iron sharpens iron; so a man sharpens the countenance of his friend."*** If you are an intercessor, encourage someone who loves praying, let them pray more, same with Choir, ushering etc get them involved. That is the team spirit. If you didn't help them get better, they might help to bring you down and you all loose it at the end of the day.

Grace Leadership approach emphasis that it becomes "*we*" and not "*I*" and replace the term "*individuals*" with "*people*" because being agile means being team-oriented.

CHAPTER THREE

==================

CHURCH LEADERSHIP PERSPECTIVES DRAWN FROM AGILE LEADERSHIP APPROACH

AGILE LEADERSHIP APPROACH (Bottom-Top Leadership Method)

Having raised the curtains, let dig in the reality of what Agile Leadership Method is all about. I want to believe that you got the concept and now understand where God is leading us.

What is Agile Leadership APPROACH (A Bottom-Up Management Approach)?

A bottom-up approach is a way of making corporate decisions that starts from the bottom of the hierarchy, rather than at the top (Waterfall/Law that's called a top-down approach). In practice, this means that the CEO/Pastor or head of the department won't be the one making all the decisions. You focus on your team needs and gather feedback from employees/workers closest to you, who are often the lowest in a traditional management hierarchy (Waterfall/Law). Agile/Grace leadership automatically improves employee/workers motivation, discover new ideas, and enhance the rate of innovation in the Organization. It flips the traditional management model upside down but doesn't eliminate Leaders/pastors/managers from the process.

In the spiritual or in the church aspect, the bottom Top approach is that which the Lord is focused on the members of the church. The owner of the Church came to give his life so he can win back the world to himself thereby calling the church The Body of Christ. If your Church/organization is experiencing Agile transformation through organizational culture and values, then Agile servant leadership is a significant leadership style that you should adopt to make the transformation successful.

What is Agile Servant Leadership?

Investopedia define servant leadership as being "*a leadership style and philosophy whereby an individual interacts with others either in a management or fellow employee capacity to achieve authority rather than power.*"

As the name is self-explanatory, servant leadership has the spirit to serve rather than to dominate. Therefore, it is totally different from the conventional waterfall style of leadership wherein there are elements of autocracy, transaction, or bureaucracy.

Hence, the philosophy of servant leader revolves around the concept of service and not power. In other words, **service is** the real power, and to serve is the real purpose of any servant leader. Meaning, that one person in their role as Servant Leader (the CEO/HOD/Pastor/Deacon etc) supports the team and serves them in a way that permits them to carry out their tasks in a self-organized way to best implement the vision according to the principles and goals of the company/organization. He is not concerned with his power or his title. In fact, he is not primarily concerned about himself, but about the team and what the team can create for the organization under ideal conditions.

Therefore, his first priority is to serve the organization, employees, and community rather than to validate its own existence. This voluntary surrender of power not only makes the team members feel more secure, it also makes them feel responsible for the success of the team and they show the corresponding commitment.

The term Servant Leadership was originally coined by Robert K. Greenleaf, the founder of the Greenleaf Center for Servant Leadership.

However, the idea of the servant leader existed ever before it was made popular by Greenleaf. It is crystal clear that our Lord Jesus Christ who is the greatest Leader the world ever known portrayed the servant leadership style all through His ministry. He lead by service and leading by service is more powerful than leading by command. He impacted His followers by doing same, he live by what He taught and that is more transforming than giving order or regulations for others to follow. With servant leadership, you lead without exhibiting direct control on the people. The corporate world has understood this and has fully adopted it. An example is where Christ demonstrated what servant leadership entailed-humility as He washed the disciple's feet to show us that a leader is first of all a servant and this is how God wants kingdom leadership to operate.

Who Is An Agile Servant Leader

A Servant Leader strives to serve others with excellence, it's seeking to deliver value and be a blessing to them in every interaction. They're grateful to God for the gifts, talents of others and they are secure in their identity by caring for those they serve and encouraging the right people in the right roles and allow them the freedom to perform. They are aware of their strengths, they willingly admit their weaknesses and mistakes and invite dissenting opinions, give credit and recognition freely. Their humility flows out of proper perspective and a grateful heart which have surrenders to God, giving Christ His rightful place as Lord, understanding that not everything depends on them, and that everything is possible with God because if we seek the approval of men over the approval of God, we'll cling to position, power, and authority for ego's sake ***Gal 1:10 "For do I now persuade [you to obey] men or God? Or do I seek to please men? if I yet pleased men, I should not be the servant of Christ".***

Jesus is a model servant Leader, ***2 Corinthians 5:15 "He died for everyone so that those who receive his new life will no longer live for themselves. Instead, they will live for Christ, who died and was raised for them"***

Agile/Grace Servant Leadership in the body of Christ.

The concept of Agile leadership in the secular world has proven to be a huge success because they are dynamic in searching for what works better. Agile is now the premier project management approach for industries and companies all over the world. The appeal lies in its simplicity and flexibility: Agile's lack of prescriptive practices makes it highly adoptable. **If you are running a business/ your life /family and you are not sensitive enough for diversity, there is a high probability that you will be stagnant. Same as if you are not flexible or well informed on changes, you will stick on the old fashion of doing things. You will be with the mentality of the 60s while people are in the 21st century. Definitely, that will slow development in your church or business.**

I will be sharing with us some vital leadership traits that the church has neglected for so long. We have already seen the loopholes of traditional or Orthodox/waterfall leadership style where by those at the top handle major decisions and the subordinates indisputably implement them. A commitment to supporting the professional and personal growth of people creates greater harmony in the organization, which is foundational to implementing business change. When articulated correctly, servant leadership is a powerful tool that can boost employee performance, enable change, and increase commitment to the organization's vision. The church cannot be redundant and static.

As aforementioned, the Bible clearly portrays the agile leadership style. It is quite evident that the philosophy of Agile servant leadership is in perfect alignment with the servant leadership attributes of Christ. Servant leadership in an agile context means the opposite of what we know (and fear) from traditional leadership. We have only been negligent to this kingdom pattern and I am calling you to be agile minded in order for us to achieve great success in the body of Christ. We also understand that the Old Testament law of Moses, is likened to the waterfall method that the world is pulling out from into the agile/Grace system.

Agile/Grace leadership approach acknowledges that anyone created by God is useful in the house of God. In the corporate governance management will feel cheated, if a duly employed and paid staff doesn't contribute in decision-making. Meaning every employee is to add value to the company. They place value on every individual and if the world will have this leadership mindset how much more the church.

How could the church believe that in a huge congregation only a handful of people can do everything? The church must wake up. You are all potential leaders, it is important for each of us to discover our area of competence and use it for the advancement of the kingdom. It is believed that each and every one of you have something eminent to contribute for the betterment of the organization and we the church should do it much better.

I term it the Agile method of Church leadership, also known as bottom-top leadership. With this system, we don't want to neglect anyone, we carry every one along and decisions making in the body of Christ must not be that of top-bottom. A typical example is the story of Naaman in the bible, a leper who has consulted the best medical facilities of his time all to no avail but his solution finally came through the instruction of young slave girl, a war captive in their house. If Naaman's wife has neglected the suggestion of this slave girl, they would have remained in their predicaments. However, they yielded to the advice of the slave girl and the result was obvious.

We should value everyone that is in the church and believe we can get council even from those younger than us in **Exodus 31:1** it is recorded that God anointing Bazeleel with the wisdom in every craftwork, the truth is that Moses least expected that Bazeleel was endowed with such talents.

Additionally, Nehemiah was more like a house manager who ran the king's palace. Though he was a rather ordinary person in a servant position, he became a transformational leader when apprised of the discontent of the Jews in Jerusalem and Judah. He prayed to God for discernment of His holy will and followed God's calling to rebuild the walls of the city of Jerusalem.

In doing so, he enacted various leadership strategies in addition to the one that came most naturally to him as a devout man of faith ranging from prayer to perseverance. He was wise, prudent, and sagacious, using those strategies; Nehemiah was able to witness the completion of his vision. The walls were restored in a mere fifty-two days.

We should therefore value everyone that God sent to us and believe that person has something positive to contribute. So it is not only about those at the top, you also matter. I know of a woman that through her diligence and hard work, has gained recognition in her field of operation such that she can recommend a worker in her domain, and authorities listen to her. There is something that made them recognized and awarded her and some of you are talented leaders, choristers, ushers etc but sit warming up the pews without being productive in the house of GOD. In **OGM,** we are allowing everyone to exhibit his or her God-given talent. If I as the Lead Pastor will allow someone to preach, it is to awaken God's ability in you and see how much such a person can reproduce what has been invested in them.

It's important to note that when we talk about bottom-up approach, it doesn't mean that the hierarchy is eliminated, neither am I sarcastic of the positional Leadership of the Church. The leadership of the Church under whose banner Christ is the head of the Church, followed by the fivefold ministries the Pastor, Evangelist, Teacher, Prophet and Apostle still stands. It has no foundation over that because when people are call into such offices, they are working directly under the covenant of Christ. In fact, in most cases, the hierarchy remains similar. What changes is the approach in decision-making.

Those lower in the hierarchy have more input in decision-making, whereas those at the top are able to look to their workers/employees for advice, information, and decision-making abilities. Meaning, those that are called into these positions will be the ones to enforce the Agile leadership mindset in members in order to encourage more workers in the vineyard. So it is not by any means to demean or underestimate the ministry gift and their offices that is the leadership of the Church.

This is something we have been doing at the end of every year, we have a yearly routine of meeting every last Sunday of the year where financial statements are submitted, deliberations and suggestions are made to the betterment of the Church against the upcoming year. This is an important aspect of agile methodology leadership. It is called a retrospective, that is to say, we see how we can become better in what we do. We identify flaws, give productive contributions, insights and solutions lay down principles to avoid repeating them. In order to keep improving, we do it often in every unit and level of leadership, some might be discontented with certain things and their approach, but with this system, they will have the avenue to express themselves.

You can't be valuable to the secular world and not be in the house of God? It is an error that at your job place you are invaluable but not the same in the church where you fellowship. ***Ephesians 2:8-9 "For by grace are all of you saved through faith; and that not of yourselves: it is the gift of God: Not of works, lest any man should boast."*** this scripture makes us understand that all that we have become is by the Grace of God, it is God's gift to us because we didn't earn it but it was granted to us. We have been given gifts and talents to advance the work of the ministry.

In the same manner, don't make a mockery of those that are in the process of working out their gift ***Titus 3:5 "Not by works of righteousness which we have***

done, but according to his mercy he saved us, by the washing of regeneration, and renewing of the Holy Spirit;" It is not by your ability that you are made righteous, that is why we call it the grace method of operating in the Church.

Consider this rhetorical question, if it is by grace and not by works, why then should I boast to be better than other? We must all come to this understanding. In applying the bottom-top method of leadership we simply mean that we are going to operate under the grace and mercy of God and be able to work as a team, our text above has said it all ***1 Corinthians 12:12- 26*** in this text of over 14 verses, we see the unity of the body, diversity encouraged, oneness and we see the ability of every member to operate in his or her God-given potential and talent. Just as a body has its different parts, so also is the church.

The corporate world came to realized is that, they invest on you not for you to add up the numbers but to add up value in order for the company to achieve its goals.

Sequel to the above, it has been irrefutably proven that the law is not a profitable approach to lead people because Jesus Christ came to change the leadership under the law. This is purely demonstrated in the scene with the woman caught in adultery. When she was brought to Jesus by the Pharisees quoting the law of Moses and were about to stone her to death Jesus justified the newly established system by calling the ones without sin to cast the first stone and when they looked at themselves they understood that none was without sin, as a result, they all dropped their stones and left, why? Because Jesus Christ came to transition the church from the old system to a new one;

Hebrews 8:6-7 "But now hath he obtained a more excellent ministry, by how much also he is the mediator of a better covenant, which was established upon better promises. For if that first covenant had been faultless, then should no place have been sought for the second".

Hebrews 8:13 "By using the term, "new," he has made the first covenant "old"; and something being made old, something in the process of aging, is on its way to vanishing altogether. He takes away the first system in order to set up the second."

Hebrews 8:6-7 "But now the work Yeshua has been given to do is far superior to theirs, just as the covenant he mediates is better. For this covenant has been given as Torah on the basis of better promises 7Indeed, if the first covenant had not given ground for faultfinding, there would have been no need for a second one"

The church also has suffered this for a while as it grew to adapt out of forceful habits or by proxy into the waterfall or law mentality form of leadership and this brought a lot of stagnancy in the church but Jesus Christ came to transition it from the law mentality of leadership to the grace mentality of leadership. When the church is shepherd or leads under the waterfall or law system, there are a lot of lapses since they have established the system where by some people are placed to head from the top to bottom, as a result some people sit on pews without participating. Meanwhile, if they are tested, it will be discovered great talent to be exploited for the good of the Church is buried in them but the law mentality has limited the opportunity for them to exhibit their gifts since they have established the system where by some people are placed to head from the top to bottom.

This brings us to the core value of this book, for those in such category, necessity is laid on me to assure you that God can equally use you, and there is something inside of you that God have been waiting for. He is waiting for that sleeping giant to be awakened and for you to start taking responsibility of things in His vineyard. You can't continue to sit passively and view it like their thing; you need to start viewing it like our thing. Stop looking down on yourself by regarding the privileged members of the congregation as indispensable. Stop undermining yourself. Stop undermining what you carry because God has honored you.

Everyone is a potential leader, and we can all be a leader wherever we are. Leadership is not only saddled on those occupying positions with title, it's the ability of anyone to influence people around him you. You don't need to be at the top to lead, it only takes influence to lead and be the voice in any field of life. Leadership is not only by position but by performance.

I say with all alacrity that in **Omega Fire Ministries** things are changing stuff to a level where all will have a say. I sold this idea to the church leadership and it was highly welcomed. The reason the church suffers from the exit of some pastors who came to the ministry already groomed and bearing the title is because they have not invested in training their people. We have to train our own and allow them to exhibit God's talents in them, then we will be amazed at the extraordinary outcome we will have.

We have gone ahead to implementing the Grace approach, as the senior Pastor, I decided that I will not be the only person to teach all four Sundays and Wednesday of the month anymore. I will pick some of the members to begin doing the work. Changes have been made in different areas, in coordination etc. and people started seeing new faces, it came as a general preparation to all the church that anyone could be called out for an assignment at any time.

CHAPTER FOUR

===============

STRENGTHS AND WEAKNESSES OF AGILE SERVANT LEADERSHIP

Strengths of Agile Servant Le*adership/Grace Leadership Method*

The bedrock of servant leadership is an altruistic calling to serve others rather than solely pursuing self-interest, that is, a selfless initiative to help without expecting a personal reward. From a leadership perspective, this call invites the leader to seek reconciliation instead of confrontation, to build a sense of community instead of tolerating separation, and to accept differences within the organization. You are wondering how a leadership model with a "serving leader" can work and what advantages it brings? Following are clear Servant Leadership advantages, so that you can support your team on the road to success.

1. Agile/Grace leadership method gives leaders the superpower to influence teams without direct authority, which allows them to drive change across the organization more effectively by

putting the leader's primary focus on people and their interactions, working in a collaborative environment, and creating value. Collaboration is the number one attributes of a successful organization. The church can be busy with so many activities, but without due collaboration it is still a fiasco. Thus, it is not worth calling it a church.

2. The Leadership culture of Agile is to focus on the betterment of others than self by creating an organization that values the human mind and heart. It eventually helps tap into people's highest creativity and productivity.

3. It Encourage and Increased Collaboration ***Philippians 2:1-4 "Therefore if there is any consolation in Christ, if any comfort of love, if any fellowship of the Spirit, if any affection and mercy, 2fulfill my joy by being like-minded, having the same love, being of one accord, of one mind. 3Let nothing be done through selfish ambition or conceit, but in lowliness of mind let each esteem others better than himself. 4Let each of you look out not only for his own interests, but also for the interests of others"*** According to a study conducted at Queen's University, 39% of employees feel a lack of collaboration in their workplace. Here, Communication will be two-way, and employees will feel empowered to

share new ideas with their managers and more people are closely involved and committed to the projects they're working on. The Bible is saying the church is to fulfill his joy by being likeminded, being in one accord, this is what God wants to see in the church, God desires us to comfort each other. There must be that love, that fellowship in the spirit, that affection for one another and same with mercy. It was one accord, unity of the Spirit that brought the presence of the Holy Spirit. The crux of the matter is to esteem one another, better than ourselves.

I am unique in my preaching style and you will not expect me to preach like some pastors you know, there are many in pastoral works who are not called to be pastors and to an extent, they have polluted the minds of some people in such a way that they criticize even those that are genuinely called to ministry. This can easily attract curse towards the person, the case of Moses should teach us a lesson, although Moses was not there when Merriam and Aaron talk against him, God revenge still fell on them. You shouldn't take someone meekness and kindness for granted, don't take someone simplicity as a weakness.

4. Agile leader serves others' needs first instead of pursuing their own self-interest and ambitions

by using empathy and persuasion rather than traditional power methods to influence people as actions are disturbed by bureaucracy and detours via hierarchical levels. The team itself makes the decisions and this enables fast and agile work, thus an increase in performance. Here, mutual help and coaching within the team are encouraged, which ensures faster and more efficient development. They actively listen to people's needs and wishes and align them with the Church/organization goals.

That is why we are encouraging diversity, it is not a one man show, when I invite external ministers, it is for us to complete each other. Grace Leadership approach in church, encourages diversity and unity.

5. Improved Employee Motivation: Statistics reveal that 89% of companies assume their staff leaves due to higher salaries, but only 12% of people end up earning more from their next company. Having more responsibility and opportunities to contribute, as advocated in a bottom-up approach makes employees feel that they have social support from their leaders and helps your team stay motivated and identify the best way to work on their projects. This model helps build trust for the leader and organization and is a key element in creating positivity, where employees express pride in being part of the organization.

6. The agile methodology in leadership solely works on Grace where God can pick anyone to use; this doesn't depend on their antecedent, how good they are etc. A case in point is Apostle Paul in the Bible; the Bible says he made havoc of the Church ***Acts 8:3 "As for Saul, he made havoc of the church...*"** He later on became an Apostle, Teacher, Pastor, Prophet and Evangelist ***2Tim 1: 10-11 "Who has saved us, and called us with an holy calling, not according to our works, but according to his own purpose and grace...Unto which I am appointed a preacher, and an apostle, and a teacher of the Gentiles." 1Tim 1:15 "This is a faithful saying, and worthy of all acceptation, that Christ Jesus came into the world to save sinners; of whom I am chief".*** This same Man who was mightily used by God told Timothy he maintained a clear conscience before God ***2Tim 1:3 "I thank God, whom I serve from my forefathers with pure conscience...*"** Grace is saying no one should be under looked.

7. Agile servant leadership does everything to develop the skills of people who are actively engaged in the organization. It creates an organization with robust and dependable teams that can take up any challenge. This form of leadership derives its sense of self from jumping into the crisis. It is ready to sacrifice its primary job of impeccable execution of the project for the instant gratification of solving the problem.

8. *Faster Innovation*: Innovation rarely comes from one person's ideas. Instead, it happens through

talking, idea-sharing, and executing on those ideas. Due to the fact that decision-making is conducted through the active participation of all the motivated individuals who are the pillars of the project, all the people feel valued and internal changes and innovation can happen faster than ever. Rather than wait for top-level management to come up with new ideas, employees will feel involved in the innovation process and actively contribute to improving services. The result is not a product of force but the product of value, belonging; passion; and labor of love.

9. Servant leadership is trained to be patient and trust the problem-solving skills of its teams. Builds a strong organization and teams that trust themselves and know how to solve problems patiently, confidently, and skillfully. This establishes a deeper sense of accountability, openness, and trust within the organization.

10. *Better Alignment*: Projects or ideas are collaboratively decided on, and employees will feel more closely aligned with the company strategy and their supervisors' expectations. This means they can go ahead and execute, confident that their work provides value to their team and company. If you're continually receiving projects from your boss, but they never discuss it with you, you're never going to

be on the same page as them. Results will never quite match your boss's expectations, as they never discussed the project with you to ensure you fully understood it or had a chance to provide constructive feedback. In fact, only 14% of employees feel confident that they're aligned with the company strategy.

11. *Promotes Trust Between Higher and Lower Level Employees*: bottom-up approach requires upper management to realize that their employees have unique knowledge, and they should be allowed to leverage it. As employees realize that their bosses value and trust their decision-making abilities, the level of trust is elevated. With trust in place, ideas can be quickly shared between upper management and lower-level employees, and feedback can be provided in honest ways, without fear of judgment.

12. *Leverage Cross-Company Knowledge*: Another key benefit of a bottom-up approach in an organization is that there won't be a reliance on one person being the only source of knowledge. If that person takes a day off, suddenly there's no one there to answer questions. With a bottom-up approach, everyone in the company becomes an essential source of knowledge, in the areas where they specialize.

Weaknesses of a Bottom-Up Management Approach

Even though, bottom-up approaches are becoming more popular, as you would expect, there are aspects of the bottom-up approach to company management that have their drawbacks.

1. Lengthier Decision Making Process: In a bottom-up approach, some decisions might still take longer. A bottom-up approach would end up slowing some projects down as more people can provide input. Top-level managers or the CEO won't make a decision and then inform their team. Instead, more people are involved, and in some cases, the process will take longer. If there aren't any changes to the speed of decision-making, it's likely that your bottom-up approach isn't genuinely bottom-up.

However, a bottom-up approach may not work for every circumstance. Someone always has the final say to ensure projects match the direction a company is moving in. Your team needs to be aware of that. If your work is time-sensitive, then a top-down approach may help you get things completed on time and without complications. Individuals and teams can quickly make improvements and suggest new projects that they're confident are in line with company goals, rather than waiting for someone in the upper-management team to suggest it.

If you're not comfortable with the new knowledge that a bottom-up approach will bring out of your employees, then you could consider having some projects managed in a top-down way, and others with a bottom-up approach to see which works more effectively. You can combine it with a top-down hierarchy, as long as you ensure employees are empowered to share their opinions and ideas with the team without the fear of unnecessary repercussions.

However, if the church fully grasps this Agile methodology we will have a smooth administration of the ministry. It will automatically facilitate follow up among the existing members, once a member discovers the needs and began participates, none will pick offence expecting to be begged to come to the church, people step on the toes of those that have secular jobs every day, speak rudely to them but they don't abandon the job. Why then will you pick offence because it is the church? That's because you have not yet understood why you are there, you have not understood the call of God upon you. You have not yet understood how much God has bestowed upon you and what you are supposed to do. When you understand these, working in the house of God becomes a joyful thing.

We need to come to that place where we beat all limitations and become participants of the work. This is where corporate America is shifting to. Nine out of ten companies are transiting from waterfall to Agile methodology because when you work as an agilist everyone in your team counts, everybody matters, they all become team players thus, rendering them more effective. No one is to be left behind, in the corporate schools in America, President Bush Junior, signed a decree of no child left behind and that's what am bringing to the church, no member left behind. Every member has the grace to effect change and can influence and change the lives of others.

CHAPTER FIVE

====================

HOW TO TRANSFORM CHURCH LEADERSHIP FROM WATERFALL TO AGILE SYSTEM

Introduction:

Leadership skill is the backbone of our very existence. The phenomenon of leadership starts with oneself and extends to all the other areas of human affairs. The philosophy of Agile servant leadership lends a new dimension to this inherent human skill of leadership. Senior leaders don't understand nature of Agile development in a true sense and beat the team with their waterfall mindset.

Transitioning from waterfall, law system to Agile which is Grace is not easy, even in the bible, Apostle Paul's revelation was difficult for others to digest, example the Church in ***Galatians 3:1-3 "O foolish Galatians, who has bewitched you, that all of you should not obey the truth, before whose eyes Jesus Christ has been evidently set forth, crucified among you? This only would I learn of you, Received all of you the Spirit by the works of the law, or by the hearing of faith? Are all of you so foolish? Having begun in the Spirit, are all of you now made perfect by the flesh?"***

It must have been a major challenge for Moses to get Pharaoh and the leadership of Israel to buy into the idea of the imminent change that would see the mould being broken and the Israelites being released from years of slavery.

It must have been difficult for the Egyptians, who realized that they would now have to learn skills. This created a crisis. Every time a change is imminent, it brings about all kinds of crisis in an organization. So this transition is not a day work because there are some strongholds in the minds of men that might have been held for years and needs to be patiently pulled down. So if you desire a change let it go by the spirit of God.

Before Leaders can influence and encourage other, leaders must unlearn their style of working and adopt new age methodology with open mind. Most of the senior leaders grew in the world where they mastered Waterfall Leadership system (1990s and early 2000) and were proud to deliver many successful projects. The question is "*are leaders really able to let go their style and preference of leadership*". Many times they struggle because many leaders still remain in old school of thoughts of Waterfall model. With such mindset, it results into expectation mismatch.

Teams do hesitate to try out different possibilities and options to solve a problem, thus limiting their innovative capabilities because of prevailing culture of reprimand when things go wrong. Leaders should help to promote open culture and not penalizing team if they have tried different approach and have not succeeded. Certainly, every attempt goes a long way and adds to team's learning and growth. It is obvious that project teams can deliver more when there is less intervention, open culture, innovative mindset and team is allowed to take decisions by mutually agreeing on scope to be delivered in each sprint. Leaders should play role of enablers rather than limiting team's innovative culture. Together they succeed because workers are excited to work in open and transparent environment. It comes to mindset change and change in our traditional approach from top to bottom.

May the Lord grace you to accept this transition, it may hurts others but God grace is available, welcome to the grace way of leadership, where we encourage, collaborate, work as a team and produce outstanding results. May the Lord break every pride in us and humble us to esteem others better than self collaborate to meet the needs of each other and see the kingdom of God advance on earth. We pray your department, church, ministry etc. is revolutionized and just as the corporate world has transitioned in agile system so shall the church exceed in Jesus Christ Name.

There can be many ways to achieve this agile transformation. However, the first and the foremost, and absolutely non-negotiable, is to have a kind of leader who has a mindset of a true servant leader. It is essential to have well-trained and spirited servant leaders with the intellectual and political culture of Agile.

Steps to Implement Agile Transformation through Servant Leadership

The change process begins when a leader starts actively listening and identifying people's needs. Nehemiah paid close attention to his followers' needs and was tenacious in accomplishing his goals. He listened to the voice of the people and showed care for their situation by humbly identifying with them. It was in terms of "we" and "us". He came to understand and identify with ***"the trouble we are in" Nehemiah 2:17.*** This first stage prepares employees to accept the change that will result in breaking the existing status quo and building up a new paradigm. The key to leadership change is foresight by predicting the near future, leaders develop a compelling vision message that shows people why the current workflow cannot continue and to develop this message, they must use their empathy and knowledge about people's needs.

That's a big deal, because resistance to change is natural and too much will derail all efforts. Involving people in the process will give them a sense of ownership. This is usually a difficult and hectic period and your servant leadership style needs some more time, patience, and practice so that the highest organizational and individual potential can be tapped into. And, when there is a will, there is always a way!

Servant leadership skills help Leaders to prevent or counteract resistance to change. By cultivating a mindset to serve others in their leadership practices, Leaders are better equipped to prepare their teams to change. Spreading the servant attitude is usually the hardest step to make, but the overall benefits for the Agile environment are enormous processes are conducted in a structured and empathetic approach that involves and empowers both teams and individuals. By applying the servant leadership framework for organizational change, leaders can successfully manage the transformation process. When people recognize that leaders respond to their needs, they are more likely to embrace and support these changes.

So a servant leader needs to find ways to emotionally heal people. Transmitting the confidence that people's needs will be met is the first step to building momentum for change. In order to overcome psychological distress, servant leaders assist followers by:

- Actively listening to people's frustrations so they can create time and space for self-awareness and communication of their needs
- Taking action to address people's needs and delivering the necessary changes; injecting positivity

- Communicating a clear change vision and goals to set the right expectations and to provide structure for employees.
- Identifying people's strengths and skills, giving positive feedback on their virtues
- Showing people how to apply their virtues to overcome challenges that will move the organization one step closer to its vision
- Helping people to build and commit to action plans with achievable deliverables in the short term
- Organizational stewardship alludes to the willingness of both leaders and teams to take responsibility for the wellbeing of the organization. Positively reinforce new behaviors by recognizing and celebrating changes

Many of these actions derive from a leader's wisdom as they become aware of their own and their team's emotions and desires. The servant leader leverages this knowledge to make well-informed, conscious decisions about the change process.

A servant leader influences people, this means persuading them to adopt a new mindset. Persuasion makes a clear distinction between the traditional leader-first (Waterfall) and servant leadership models (Grace). Servant leaders make people feel that it was they who made a decision or participated in the decision-making, rather than having it imposed by an authority.

IMPLEMENTATION PROCESS

There are many people occupying positions, but true leadership is sadly missing. Churches will rise and fall based on who is leading and the style of leadership employed. If turnaround is needed in a church the first issue that must be addressed is that of leadership. The kind of leaders that will bring restoration to the church must be dynamic, complement, spiritually able, courageous, prayerful, risk-taking and focused leader because not every leader is prepared and ready for such hurricane task. The associate leaders are equally important. They must be loyal, truthful and supportive to God and the Pastor. A typical example is Nehemiah, which in the last paragraph of this section will be expounded.

Perhaps leaders that could resist the change, stand as enemies of the progress and lead the church down are around, then they should be wisely and boldly removed, so that, the new leader can have freehand to demonstrate his ideas, visions, and pick close associates. Leadership change will bring fresh momentum, zeal and purpose to the church. New ideas and commitment will spring forth and things will start looking up gradually. Following are some attributes to consider:

The Leader must be committed to Excellence. That is the mindset of going for quality in everything and every area, going for nothing but the best. It must not be policy decision only, but also a mindset, an attitude and a way of thinking and behaving in the church and this is attained not merely by demanding excellence, but by modeling it. Be the best of it and lead yourself extremely well, Loyalty will be earned when people see that you are truly an example of what you are challenging them to do and become. Excellency in the church does not just happen, it is made to happen. Excellence within will reflect in the outside as in the way of doing things in leadership, worship, preaching, printing, publications, facilities management, media, spiritual life, evangelism etc. Mediocre and ramshackle ways of doing things must be completely jettisoned. With Agile leadership approach, turn around will become a reality in the ministry.

It is practically impossible to re-invest a church without change. To turn around the downward spiral of a church demands for radical change from the old ways of doing things; we must totally welcome and embrace change. If change is detested, viewed with alarm and resisted, it will continue on the downward slope. But if change is welcomed and embraced, then growth will be evident. The leaders that will renew the church must function as agents of change and must not be afraid of changing old, archaic and out molded way of doing things. Not all changes will bring growth but there can be no growth without change.

Training and Discipleship: Leadership by today's terms requires some degree of training and discipleship in order for it to be effective. Training communicates love, acceptance, assurance and loyalty in the people, there must be proper training to harness the deposits of God in the people so as to contribute their own quota to the advancement of the kingdom. Many have found themselves, accepting, ascending, or delegated to positions of leadership, possibly on grounds of longevity in their church and place of work. Some are those who came into the church/organization through the doors of influence and connection.

As noted by Peter Wagner, a positive Pastor is the first vital sign of a healthy church. A pastor who is a possibility thinker and whose dynamic leadership has been proven is a healthy sign for the church. The person and personality or a pastor goes a long way to determine the health of the church.

Open Opportunities for Leadership: There shouldn't be any barrier of ministry opportunity for people. The gifts and ministry of people are greatly oppressed by some leaders. The immaturity of some leaders flounders the church, i.e. the inability of the leaders to handle the growth and expansion of the church fear, jealousy, envy and oppression of subordinates, while in others it is some moral laxity by the leaders. Where there are no open opportunities for the expression of the grace and gifts of God in their lives, the church will never maximize growth and the leadership that is jealous and envious of the gifts, endowments and special calling of its people cannot but experience mass breaks away.

Wisdom will help the leader to conceptualize and define the building blocks of change, while persuasion will opens the door to engaging people by encouraging them to propose new initiatives and commit to the ones that have been agreed upon.

Strategies of Handling Opponents to the Work

The leader must know he or she has enemies who don't like to lift the burden of the people up; who hate the progress the leader implements. So what do you do? You are very careful and watchful at all times. You make your trust completely in God, not in human beings because you don't know what is in their thoughts and hearts, Nehemiah 4:9. He and his people had many enemies and opponents and the way he handle those opponents was simply splendid.

Immediately the rumor spread that someone came to rebuild the walls of Jerusalem, the enemies of Judah who did not want Jerusalem rebuilt began to attack Nehemiah. The enemies discouraged the people and even those among the Jews who were there before. They ridiculed and mocked him. Their enemies did everything possible to discourage them, send threats, layed false allegations and plots against him. However, Nehemiah answered them by taking the problem to God, and as well encouraged the people to trust and have faith in God rather than listening to the opponent. He knew he was "doing a great work" (6:3) and could not come down from the wall to debate with the enemies. That tells us that we shouldn't waste our time responding to critics.

"Then answered I them, and said unto them, the God of heaven, he will prosper us, therefore we his servants will arise and build., but you have no portion, no right, no memorial in Jerusalem." Nehemiah 2:20; 4:4 "Be not afraid of them. Remember the Lord which is great and terrible and fight for your brethren and sons and your daughters and your houses." Nehemiah 4:14

A man was hired to kill him and when he was threatened that someone was going to kill him, he remained courageous in face of threats & enemies. He responded thus;

"***Should, such a man as I flee, and who is there and being as I am will go into the temple to save his life." Nehemiah 6: 11.*** Here was a man who was not afraid of threats or plots. Why? He knew the Almighty GOD was in control of his life and events.

No enemy will destroy or hurt him as long as he was obedient and doing God's will. God controls events in life, the bible says He "GOD" rules in the affairs of men. However, not arrogant and envious men and women. God will protect him from the enemies because he was doing the right thing for his people and that was God's desire. Likewise you, God protect the leader doing the right thing, and whose motive is right. Nehemiah discerned the man was hired to kill him, and he refused to meet with the man. The leader who loves God is filled with God's wisdom, insight and divinely protected. He or she also hears from the voice of the Holy Spirit to know what to do at all time, and what not to do.

Furthermore, Nehemiah's first line of defense against adversaries was prayer. The entire restructuring of Jerusalem was enveloped in the power of prayer. His work was accomplished through an active prayer life, role modeling, adaptability, and foresight. Nehemiah faith and hope was embedded in God. What makes rulers and powerful men in Jerusalem to listen to him? Nehemiah was nothing. This was because he was a leader who had already prevailed with God in prayer, brought God to the situation, and the people listened to him. It was not because of his eloquence, or endowment, or natural talent only, but because of his prevailing life- power with God in prayer.

He knew the God of Israel what He can do, he was confident that this God was in control and can do all things through him. His faith was not in people, but in the God of Israel. No enemy, or rulers, or people hired could touch him or kill him. He became invisible because of his absolute trust and faith in the Lord. "*No weapon formed against the believer shall prosper.*" This kind of faith and trust in the Lord gives you peace, confidence and free you from all anxiety and fears.

Agile Approach Ceremonies And Their Relevance To The Church

They are four official ceremonies which are important elements of the agile leadership strategy. They are not just meetings for the sake of having meetings. Rather, these ceremonies provide the framework for teams to plan, track and get work done in a structured manner, also help to set expectations, empower the team to collaborate effectively, and ultimately drive results. These are done by engaging stakeholders with their work and help them reflect on how well they've worked together. It provides a framework for cross-functional teams to solve complex challenges. When managed correctly, the ceremonies support high levels of productivity and effective communication and between the project team and its stakeholders, if not handled properly, it can drown out the value they are intended to provide. The meetings have defined lengths, frequencies, and goals. In other words, these ceremonies exist to make delivering possible. Without further ado, let's dive in.

The four scrum ceremonies are: **Sprint Planning, Daily Scrum, Sprint Review, Sprint Retrospective and Backlog Refinement which I'll include due to the importance for our study.**

SPRINT PLANNING

Sprint Planning is the scrum ceremony designed to make sure the team is prepared to get the right things done every sprint.

The meetings set out precisely what the team will accomplish during the sprint, it happens at the beginning of a new scrum sprint and is designed for the Product Owner and Development Team to meet and review the prioritized product backlog for the next two weeks Sprint through a series of discussions and negotiations. They size the stories, and give room for each developer to pick what stories they will love to work on. Stories are used to build customers' request, it can be broken up into smaller tasks and assigned during sprint planning so that everyone knows what they're held accountable to.

A successful sprint planning ceremony will address and answer these three critical questions:

- Why does this sprint matter?
- What can be done during this sprint?
- How will the chosen work get done?

How is Sprint Planning Applicable to The Church?

How Sprint Planning is applicable to the church is that it is regarded as a planning done by each department on what they will love to do to grow the church. e.g. At the beginning of each year, the Pastor or the Leader gives achievable tasks to each department respectively, something like Evangelism department is given "operation win a soul in the next three days and so on when different department meets". It is expected that each department of the church goes to plan how to accomplish such task or achieve that goal.

Before the sprint planning session, the team should develop a sprint goal on evangelism and then update relevant user stories and prioritize the product backlog.

Then, the department team works together to discuss each item and estimates how much effort will be required to complete them.

The department team is to decide how much they can realistically get the job done and adds those tasks to their sprint backlog. Encourage the team to sketch out tasks, bugs, and any item that requires it during this meeting. It should be an extremely collaborative ceremony/meeting.

DAILY SCRUM OR DAILY STAND UP: This ceremony provides a frequent opportunity for the team to get together and communicate individual progress toward the sprint goal. This is the first thing every Scrum team does in the morning. They get together, define a plan for the day's work, and identify any blockers. Each developer tells the team what he did yesterday and what he or she will be working on today and it illuminate any impediments that are slowing the team's progress.

During this ceremony, each member of the Department Team should briefly answer the following questions:

- ✓ What did you do yesterday?
- ✓ What will you do today?
- ✓ Are there any impediments in the way?

Hold the meeting at the same time each day of the week (typically in the mornings), and do what you can to make this as routine for the team as possible

How is Daily Stand Up Relevant for The Church?

Here is an example relevant for the Church today. I call it our daily meditation and prayers to God couple with briefing by the team. This meeting enables the team to be sync, build intimacy with God and trust with each other. The team would hold each other accountable for achieving their commitments on a daily basis. They share visibility of how the sprint is progressing and the most important element is to highlight if there is anything getting in their way and the Pastor or HOD is responsible for clearing these roadblocks for the Department Team so they can focus on delivering the work identified in Sprint Planning. During the Daily meeting, every member typically answers some of these three questions:

- ✓ What did you complete yesterday that helped the team meet the sprint goal?
- ✓ What will you do today to help the team meet the sprint goal?
- ✓ Is anything blocking your progress or hindering you to help the team meet the sprint goal?

There's implicit accountability in reporting what work you completed yesterday in front of your peers. No one wants to be the team member who is constantly doing the same thing and not making progress. With a daily review of the team's progress, everyone stays motivated and aware of the sprint's progress.

SPRINT REVIEW:

Sprint Review is the scrum ceremony where the result of all work completed during a particular sprint can be showcased to the key stakeholders and progress toward the product goal is discussed.

At the conclusion of each sprint, the Sprint Review provides a platform for the Departmental Team to showcase all of the work that has been completed. This allows stakeholders to see things sooner than later and inspect the outcome of the sprint or adapt the product as it emerges or determine next actions.

Sprint Reviews of work completed can be conducted in a Demo nature or can be set up to be more structured.

How it is Relevant to the Church

It is relevant to the church today in the sense that it is a yard stick to measure departmental achievable goals. It is the most direct way for early and frequent feedback to be collected and eventually added to the product backlog. E.g. A particular department showcase a report on the success of a target that was given them by the church leader, let's say a target to win one million soul and this number of souls were won within this sprint(time frame), our target was to feed people, we fed this number of people. A general feedback into what you accomplish during that sprint. It is also a period of assessment of the job that was supposed to be done. Do everything you can to let the team shine. Most importantly, all of the work showcased during this time should be fully demonstrable and meet the team's quality bar to be considered complete. The team should feel empowered to show off the work they've been able to complete over the course of the sprint and get immediate feedback from project stakeholders (the Church/company's leaders) that can be implemented in the next sprint.

THE SPRINT RETROSPECTIVE:

The Sprint Retrospective; Sprint Retrospective should be the final scrum ceremony in the sequence that is specifically designed to help the team better. It allows the team to look back on the work that was just completed, illuminate recommendations to be better and mitigate risk moving forward.

After a Sprint Review has been done, the team needs to have the opportunity to reflect on the work that was just showcased and share challenges and discuss ways in which to improve. The sprint retrospective is that ceremony which gives the team a platform to discuss things that are roadblocks, those that are going well, things that could go better, and some suggestions for changes. These are the common questions to be asked:

- ✓ What went well over the previous sprint?
- ✓ What didn't go so well? the roadblocks getting on the way of the work
- ✓ What could we do differently to improve?

Sprint retrospectives can be challenging because they require the project team to honestly appraise how well they're working together. However, this ceremony should provide a blameless and safe space for members of the team to openly provide their honest feedback and recommendations for improvements. It should drive change. All actionable feedback should be collected and assigned so that members of the team understand who is responsible for what.

While the Retrospective may sound similar to the Sprint Review, it focuses on reviewing the work of the team instead of the progress of the project. The goal is to optimize for quality and productivity which is essential, as continuous improvement is a core principle of Agile. During the ceremony, understand what worked and what didn't in the last sprint, with a focus on increasing quality and effectiveness. That is focusing on the parts of the process that are working well and identify areas of weakness that may need to improve.

As a team leader, be sure to coach the team to provide honest feedback & be respectful throughout the course of the ceremony. Focus on collaboration rather than competition and gather data and find out what's working so the team can continue to focus on those areas. Also, find out what's not working and use the time to find creative solutions and develop an action plan. Continuous improvement is what sustains and drives development within an agile team, and retrospectives are a key part of that.

How it is Relevant to the Church:

It is relevant for today's church because you have to keep up with what's going on regularly! Let's learn something from that. Doesn't have to be daily, or weekly but regularly keeping up with the team of people helping to keep programs running smoothly will help the entire church as church leaders and volunteer teams are working toward the same goals.

Retrospective is the idea that what has happened can be improved, tweaked, or expanded to create a better outcome. Every leadership team can implement this principle today. It costs nothing to have a discussion and planning opportunity by reviewing the previous outcomes of plans. It takes very little time to get everyone together and have these meaningful discussions.

Church sits either quarterly, annually or biannually to review all they have done within the time frame. Some Churches call it business meetings. For example, our choir department is to weekly hold retrospective conversations with the team, and as the team members gets the hang of sharing open and honest feedback on what didn't work or what can be improved upon the ideas and improvements can begin happening on a more regular basis where team members aren't waiting for quarterly or yearly meetings to talk about these things. What our choir does is to replay the precedent praise and worship session, identify their mistakes and amend for subsequent services. As a result, our choir has never remained the same again; we have drastically improved and keep improving. This can be implemented departmentally, by the church at their own convenience. Here every body have a say before only two or three were picked to speak but with agile approach, everybody have a say, e.g. men, women, young adult etc. The value of idea and team building and discussions on what did and didn't work is limitless.

Then, ask each person on the team to provide their insights on:

- ✓ How they felt the previous went.
- ✓ What went well during the sprint?
- ✓ What worked or didn't work and could we have done better during the sprint?
- ✓ What are our next steps for the coming sprint?
- ✓ What can we change? So you can avoid repeating the same mistake.

Make it a safe place for the team to honestly and openly reflect on the team progress, team process, and team health and come up with specific steps to improve blockers and pain points and also celebrate their successes.

Additionally, it could also be viewed as a retreat where the body withdraws for a time of renewal of strength. The bible says in ***Isaiah 40:31"But they that wait upon the LORD shall renew their strength; they shall mount up with wings as eagles; they shall run, and not be weary; and they shall walk, and not faint".*** it is imperative that once a while departments take such sprint ceremony in order to make greater exploit. So it is biblical. Nevertheless, the church can pick the model that best suites them. These are the areas of retrospective and this lead us to the final one the Backlog refinement.

Backlog refinement:

Though this 5th one is not always listed as an "official agile" ceremony, refining your backlog is an essential part of keeping your team efficient and effective. Product backlog refinement is the list of tasks and issues that your team wants to complete in future sprints. But because Agile is based on rapid feedback, these issues can become outdated or change in priority. Therefore, there is need of continuous process of cleaning up, adjusting, and updating your task and feature list, this is called backlog refinement. Some teams set specific period to go through and clean up the backlog, while others do it continuously throughout each sprint.

It is the act of breaking down and further defining Product Backlog items into smaller, more precise items. This is an ongoing activity to add details, such as a description, order, and size. Attributes often vary with the domain of work. - The Scrum Guide

During Backlog Refinement, you should start by looking at your full list of issues either on your product roadmap or by filtering them by trackers, milestones, or priority. You add more and more details to your Backlog items by moving your most important tasks and issues to the top of your list, so that they're in great shape when you pick candidates for the next sprint during Sprint Planning.

A well-prioritized and organized backlog makes all other agile ceremonies easier. The goal of these sessions is to use your latest knowledge and feedback to update your backlog, rewrite user stories, and prioritize tasks.

Here is how the session is relevant for the Church. For example at the beginning of the year, a Pastor /visionary or Leader, goes before the Lord to inquire on what or how the Lord wants him to handle the ministry for that year. So after receiving, he communicates to the associate pastor for implement-tation.

For session, you put down the vision before the Church leadership and begin analyzing it according to ***Habakkuk 2:2 "And the LORD answered me, and said, Write the vision, and make it plain upon tables, that he may run that readeth it."***

When the pastor received inspiration from the Lord and wrote it down, it was not in an organized manner. The moment the vision of the church for that year is written down and everything needed is outlined, during this session, the entire church will deliberate on it, how they can use it for the advancement of the kingdom and set them in order of their priorities. Those details may include a clear User Story, Acceptance Criteria and estimated effort.

From there, they start implementing them by bringing them to the sprint backlog in their respective department.

The Twelve Agile Manifesto Principles

The Twelve Principles are the guiding principles for the methodologies that are included under the title "The Agile Movement." They describe a culture in which change is welcome, and the customer is the focus of the work. They also demonstrate the movement's intent as described by Alistair Cockburn, one of the signatories to the Agile Manifesto, which is to bring development into alignment with business needs.

As a church leader, how can you harness the principles of Agile to improve the church's departments? Are you meeting people's needs? Are you able to respond to a changing culture? Agile speaks to all these issues and provides a framework to bring people closer to each other and closer to God. Culture is constantly changing. As it shifts, churches feel the need to change. The leadership often knows they need to flexibly make some adjustments, but many times they don't follow through because, let's face it, change is h*ard. But it's important.*

The twelve principles of agile development and it's relevance to the Church are as follo*ws:*

Customer satisfaction through early and continuous software delivery - Customers are happier when they receive working software at regular intervals, rather than waiting extended periods of time between releases.

Accommodate changing requirements throughout the development process - The ability to avoid delays when a requirement or feature request changes.

This is welcoming changes to existing plans, adjusting plans to fit needs in shorter periods of time. Essentially it is FLEXIBILITY. Churches need to be more flexible.

Your church has to change drastically to be able to meet the needs of the people. The churches that adapted early and often in a very flexible way kept more members tuning in. Churches that failed to find ways to stay "open" to their congregation virtually or otherwise lost some Christians. Flexibility and a sense of community are essential

Frequent delivery of working software - Scrum accommodates this principle since the team operates in software sprints or iterations that ensure regular delivery of working software.

Collaboration between the business stakeholders and developers throughout the project - Better decisions are made when the business and technical team are aligned.

This principle seems to be the most overlooked by churches today. I understand, we are all busy, and many church leadership teams are made up of volunteers who have kids, full time jobs, and activities. Though it is not enough to forgo church leadership teams regular meeting, it is imperative to stay on the same page and check in with each other on their areas of leadership. Tight-knit teams are going to be more successful, not just for accountability but to keep cohesive strategy moving forward.

Support, trust, and motivate the people involved – Motivated teams are more likely to deliver their best work than unhappy teams.

Projects are built around motivated individuals, who have won trust, and who should be trusted in Agile is key. Those who love what they are doing and want to further the mission of the church will come up with good ideas to further it. Trust them to try out some of those ideas with the buy-in from the whole team but the idea of trust often comes with time. Church leaders can help teams cultivate a sense of trust and expand ideas by having those regular check-ins and challenging team members to come up with new ideas on how to implement those ideas. Let those team members passionate about good ideas step up and run the ideas.

Here's an example a church could use today: Say a team member has a new idea for a community group, like feeding the poor. Maybe a team member wants to step up and create the group, help run it, and create events to keep the group running smoothly with the purpose of offering church-agreed-upon activities. Perhaps the pastor doesn't need to be fully involved but an elder and a group of volunteers can run it.

Maybe there's buy-in from the whole team and anyone who wants to help execute the idea can pitch in. This example can be used for any idea, whether its singles and unmarried group to foster Christ centered relationship, activity for teens and children ministry to get them engaged in the church. Whatever the idea, the most passionate and engaged idea bearer will help create a level of success that may not be as vast without that idea person.

Enable face-to-face interactions - Communication is more successful when development teams are co-located.

The best form of communication is Conversation and communication is KEY to any great relationship and that includes team communication. The more, the better.

Microsoft tool helps team to keep conversations on-going including Google Meet, Skype, Go To Meeting, and etc. help when those meetings can't happen in person. It important to have a way to keep communication open to teams.

Working software is the primary measure of progress - Delivering functional software to the customer is the ultimate factor that measures progress.

Agile processes to support a consistent development pace - Teams establish a repeatable and maintainable speed at which they can deliver working software, and they repeat it with each release.

Attention to technical detail and design enhances agility - The right skills and good design ensures the team can maintain the pace, constantly improve the product, and sustain change.

Simplicity - Develop just enough to get the job done for right now because the art of maximizing the amount of work not done is most essential.

Churches who take time to simplify processes, as well as getting back to basics on the purpose of programs, tasks, teams, etc. benefit greatly.

There's always a way to simplify multi-step processes and projects. You just have to look wider and deeper at times to find the ways to simplify. It's well worth everyone's time to think through the processes periodically in order to all agree simplicity is a key principle you all want and watch your work decrease, or what your efficiency increases.

Self-organizing teams encourage great architectures, requirements, and designs. The best emerge from self-organizing teams

Regularly Reflect and Adjust Your Way of Work to Boost Effectiveness - Skilled and motivated team members who have decision-making power, take ownership, communicate regularly with other team members, and share ideas that deliver quality products. In order to achieve this, at regular intervals, the team reflects on how to become more effective, then tunes and adjusts its behavior accordingly.

The idea of reflecting on adjusting procedures and processes based on successes or failures is common. We do this all the time in our life experiments. A church may hold a new event, see if people enjoy it and it achieves the goals set and reevaluates where that event can improve. This principle is something some do automatically as they think about what to plan next.

You will never regret the process of looking at each element of your church and evaluating whether or not there are places or elements that can be improved through the lens of your goals and abilities.

Dearly Beloved if you read the above twelve principles carefully, you will discover that they give more value to Man than on Machines, They also give more value to Customer Satisfaction, Accommodating Change, collaboration between business stakeholder or owners.

It is obvious that such principles are biblically base though it might not be common in the body of Christ. I am thrilled how the leadership of Jesus and the launch of the early church align with such ideas. Simple, gifts-based, and constantly improving on ourselves have marked us from the beginning. Jesus, the disciples knew what was important because of that, they refused many good things that were of secondary importance.

Wise leaders should emulate Jesus, before launching out into the specifics of implementation. As a result, the best future plans are lean, simple, and assume that much of the work of specific ministries and initiatives will be revealed along the way. That agility is at the heart of relevance and nimbleness for churches and work places in the 21st century.

The Four Values of The Agile Manifesto

The Agile Manifesto is comprised of four foundational values and 12 supporting principles which lead the Agile approach to software development. Each Agile approach applies the four values in different ways, but all of them rely on them to guide the development and delivery of high-quality, working software.

How can you take these values and apply them to your own mission? Becoming more agile as a congregation, will increase your productivity and make your church more effective for the kingdom of God.

1. **Individuals and Interactions Over Processes and Tools:**

   The first value in the Agile Manifesto is "Individuals and interactions over processes and tools." Valuing people more highly than processes or tools is easy to understand because it is the people who respond to business needs and drive the development process. If the process or the tools drive development, the team is less responsive to change and less likely to meet customer needs. Communication is an example of the difference between valuing individuals versus process. In the case of individuals, communication is fluid and happens when a need arises. In the case of process, communication is scheduled and requires specific content.

Matthew 22:36-40 "Master, which is the great commandment in the law? [37]Jesus said unto him, Thou shalt love the Lord thy God with all thy heart, and with all thy soul, and with all thy mind. [38]This is the first and great commandment. [39]And the second is like unto it, Thou shalt love thy neighbour as thyself. [40]On these two commandments hang all the law and the prophets.

Beholding the above four values, there is no doubt that everything looks as an inspiration from the Bible. Just consider the first one that says Individual Interaction Over Processes and Tools. That is talking about placing More Value on people more highly than processes or tools is easy to understand because it is the people who respond to business needs and drive the development process. Here Christ was focus on the people more than himself. His interest was to see people free.

2. Working Software Over Comprehensive Documentation

Historically, enormous amounts of time were spent on documenting the product for development and ultimate delivery. Technical specifications, technical requirements, technical prospectus, interface design documents, test plans, documentation plans, and approvals required for each. The list was extensive and was a cause for the long delays in development. Agile does not eliminate documentation, but it streamlines it in a form that gives the developer what is needed to do the work without getting bogged down in minutiae. Agile documents requirements as user stories, which are sufficient for a software developer to begin the task of building a new function.

The Agile Manifesto values documentation, but it values working software more.

James 2:14-16, What doth it profit, my brethren, though a man say he hath faith, and have not works? can faith save him? [15]If a brother or sister be naked, and destitute of daily food, [16]And one of you say unto them, Depart in peace, be ye warmed and filled; notwithstanding ye give them not those things which are needful to the body; what doth it profit?

Looking at the second value, it says Working Software Over Comprehensive Documentation. What this teaches us that are in the Church is that the Cooperate world wants to see results than just having big documents. They need action than grand planning. To the Church what is needful is the action, that is seeing the physical Manifestation of God power than just telling people Religious and things of what happened in Bible days. Apostle Paul told the Corinthians in ***1 Corinthians 2:4" and neither the delivery nor the content of my message relied on compelling words of "wisdom" but on a demonstration of the power of the Spirit, so that your trust might not rest on human wisdom but on God's power.***"

3. **Customer Collaboration Over Contract Negotiation**

Negotiation is the period when the customer and the product manager work out the details of a delivery, with points along the way where the details may be renegotiated. Collaboration is a different creature entirely. With development models such as Waterfall, customers negotiate the requirements for the product, often in great detail, prior to any work starting. This meant the customer was involved in the process of development before development began and after it was completed, but not during the process. The Agile Manifesto describes a customer who is engaged and collaborates throughout the development process, making. This makes it far easier for development to meet their needs of the customer. Agile methods may include the customer at intervals for periodic demos, but a project could just as easily have an end-user as a daily part of the team and attending all meetings, ensuring the product meets the business needs of the customer.

John 6:3-13 "And Jesus went up into a mountain, and there he sat with his disciples. [13]Therefore they gathered them together, and filled twelve baskets with the fragments of the five barley loaves, which remained over and above unto them that had eaten."

The third says Customer Collaboration Over Contract Negotiation. From the above verse, we see Our Lord Jesus Christ collaborating and the result is evident in verse thirteen. We should Collaborate with the congregation over following institutional church division.

What that is saying is that Pastors should Value Church Members than their Titles. In other words Value New Church Members and create adequate time with them than saying the Pastor is not available because that member in New to the Church. That means, as a pastor, avail yourself to both great and small.

4. **Responding to Change Over Following a Plan**

Traditional software development regarded change as an expense, so it was to be avoided. The intention was to develop detailed, elaborate plans, with a defined set of features and with everything, generally, having as high a priority as everything else, and with a large number of many dependencies on delivering in a certain order so that the team can work on the next piece of the puzzle.

With Agile, the shortness of an iteration means priorities can be shifted from iteration to iteration and new features can be added into the next iteration. Agile's view is that changes always improve a project; changes provide additional value.

Perhaps nothing illustrates Agile's positive approach to change better than the concept of Method Tailoring, defined in An Agile Information Systems Development Method in use as: "A process or capability in which human agents determine a system development approach for a specific project situation through responsive changes in, and dynamic interplays between contexts, intentions, and method fragments." Agile methodologies allow the Agile team to modify the process and make it fit the team rather than the other way around.

Mark 2:17 "***When Jesus heard it, he saith unto them, They that are whole have no need of the physician, but they that are sick: I came not to call the righteous, but sinners to repentance.***"

The fourth is more important to me. It says Responding to Change Over Following a Plan, Agile Management is an incremental approach to planning. Agility is what is desperately needed in much of congregational life. This is to tell us that the Church should be let by the Holy Spirit than to hold on to Old traditions that are working in this twenty-first century, rather they should respond to the changing needs of the people. Be flexible with admiration and the way things are run in the Church. The fact that we did this in a particular way 20 years ago does not mean things must remain like that for every. Traditional software development regarded change as an expense, so it was to be avoided.

The Five Scrum Values

The five Scrum values are commitment, focus, openness, respect, and courage. According to the Scrum guide, "Successful use of Scrum depends on people becoming more proficient in living these five values."

The Scrum framework was designed specifically for managing complex projects that must be able to adapt quickly to changes in scope or requirements (the scope definition in project management refers to the objectives and requirements that go into each project). That's why each of these five Scrum values is so critical to the success of a Scrum project.

Let's explore each one a little more closely:

Remove barriers, find clarity, exceed goals

Anything is possible with the most powerful work management software at your fingertips.

1. Focus everyone focuses on the work of the Sprint and the goals of the Scrum team."
   — The Scrum Guide
   One of the hallmarks of the Scrum methodology is the sprint, which is a specified period of time during which team members work to achieve a stated goal. In order to get the most out of each sprint, each team member must remain focused on the task at hand as well as how it impacts the sprint goal.

   To help team members stay focused, Scrum masters can limit the number of tasks or priorities placed on each person during sprints. Additionally, encouraging full team participation at the daily Scrum meeting can help individuals stay focused on their specified tasks.

   Any ministry that focuses on Christ, on the people, His Birth, Death and Resurrection, will always succeed. Churches and individuals have to focus on their vision and dreams and fulfill them. Christ is a typical example of a fulfilled vision ***1 John 3:8 "... The reason the Son of God was made manifest (visible) was to undo (destroy, loosen, and dissolve) the works the devil [has done]."***

Colossians 2:15 "[God] disarmed the principalities and powers that were ranged against us and made a bold display and public example of them, in triumphing over them in Him and in it [the cross"

Shift your church from an inward focus to an outward focus. If you stay focused on the people who need Jesus, you'll be more aware of the ways you have to change to reach them.

And this isn't just about how you design your services and programs. Leaders must model what it looks like to develop intentional relationships with people outside the church and outside the faith to stay in tune with a shifting culture.

1) **Openness** "The Scrum team and its stakeholders agree to be open about all the work and the challenges with performing the work." — The Scrum Guide

In order for the Scrum team to make the most progress in the shortest time possible, each team member must be brutally honest and open about their progress. The purpose of the daily Scrum meeting is to identify and solve problems. That can't happen if team members aren't forthcoming about issues or roadblocks they're experiencing. Additionally, team members must be open to working with their colleagues and view them as valuable contributors to the success of the project.

One of the best ways for Scrum masters to promote openness is by being transparent with their teams. Delivering honest feedback during daily Scrum meetings is not only vital to making necessary adjustments but will also encourage honesty and openness in return from team members.

In the other hand, when the ministry encourages openness amongst the brethren, openness to share business ideas, open to not criticize, open to accept one failure and be teachable etc. with these, success is inevitable.

2) **Respect**: Scrum team members respect each other to be capable, independent people." — The Scrum Guide

Just as it does in any team endeavor, respect in a Scrum team means recognizing that no single individual or their contribution is more valuable than another. Respect also means trusting your fellow team members to fulfill their tasks, listening to and considering their ideas, and recognizing their accomplishments.

Scrum masters can help foster respect among their teams by demonstrating respect to the product owner, stakeholders, and their team members.

These are all core values from the bible, respecting the brethren, the pastors and leaders. Respect will spark the ministry to higher height because this lacks in the body of Christ.

3) **Courage:** "The Scrum team members have courage to do the right thing and work on tough problems." — The Scrum Guide

Finally, Scrum teams must have the courage to be honest, open, and transparent both with themselves and with stakeholders about the project's progress and any roadblocks they're experiencing. Team members also need the courage to ask for help when it's needed, to try new tactics or methods they're not used to, and to respectfully disagree and have an open dialogue.

Just like respect, Scrum masters can promote courage first and foremost by demonstrating it. The Scrum master must have the courage to stand up to stakeholders and product owners to prevent mid-sprint changes or scope creep.

Meaning you shouldn't give up. Don't pull back. The bible says ***Hebrews 10:39:39 "However, we are not the kind who shrink back and are destroyed; on the contrary, we keep trusting and thus preserve our lives!"***

Knowing that God is with you and will always be there for you. Courage is one of the values that keep us going in the Faith. There will always be challenges but Courage will keep us moving.

4) **Commitment:** People personally commit to achieving the goals of the Scrum team." — The Scrum Guide

Think about an elite Special Forces military unit. These small, specialized teams are highly adaptable and must carry out complicated missions that can change in the blink of an eye. In order to successfully navigate these life and death situations, each team member must be 100% committed not only to the mission at hand but to their fellow team members, too.

While most projects are not matters of life and death, the general concept is the same for Scrum teams. Scrum teams must be able to work together as a unit to achieve a common goal. That means trusting one another to follow through on their tasks and deliver to the best of their abilities. This will only happen when each team member has fully committed to the team and the project.

Scrum masters and team leaders can help promote commitment by facilitating proper sprint planning and protecting teams from mid-sprint scope changes and unnecessary pressure from product owners. On like in our Christian Faith, commitment is the key. As we have believed the Lord Jesus Christ, it is similar to the commitment you make to your spouse. You are committed to the cause of Christ, committed to move toward and never relinquish

He is compassionate, shows sensitivity and emotional intelligence to empathize within the organization and always has an open ear for the team instead of exercising power and relying on rights that arise from a hierarchy.

CHAPTER SIX

UNDERSTANDING THE MOTIVATING POWERS OF A SERVANT- LEADER

Leadership is functional not positional. You are a leader when people follow you, even when you do not solicit it. Following are some motivating powers of a servant Leader

- ✓ *A Servant Leader Values Gods Flock*; Let them know you value them, repeatedly tell them what value they bring and by so doing motivate them to achieve more. This will also prompt other people to praise the team's efforts. Affirmation is a positive way of encouraging people to choose a particular way to live, or act. ***Acts 20:28 "Take heed therefore to yourselves, and to all the flock, in which the Holy Spirit hath appointed you bishops, to feed the church of God, which He purchased with his own blood." Psalm 78:70-72 "He also chose David His servant and took him from the sheepfolds; from the care of the ewes with suckling lambs. He brought him to shepherd Jacob His people, and***

Israel His inheritance. So he shepherded them according to the integrity of his heart, and guided them with his skillful hands"

- ✓ *A Servant Leader Does What It Takes*: I believe the true measure of leaders is not the number of people who serve them but the number of people they serve. They adopt an attitude of servant first, leader second. Everything they do is measured in light of the value it can add. They serve the mission of the church/organization and lead by serving those on the mission with them. You know that you are a leader when you are motivated by the desire to serve as a leader. It's actually very simple. You have the heart of a servant if it doesn't bother you to serve others.

- ✓ *A Leader Put Away Pride And Pretense*: We don't gain influence with others by impressing them, it is better to make mistakes than to fake perfection. People can see us for who we really are. If we make it our goal to impress them, we puff up our pride and end up being pretentious. If you want to influence others, don't try to impress them. Pride is really nothing more than a form of selfishness and pretense and it is only a way to keep people at arm's length so that they can't see who you really are. Instead of impressing others, let them impress you. He/she must leave room for people to be able to be honest with themselves and the system; that way there can be a critical analysis of what is not working, rather than a blanket acceptance of things

Regardless of status or fame, a leader must realize that he is just like the people before whom he stands. Only then can he be a true leader. It's really a matter of attitude. The people with charisma, those who attract others to themselves, are individuals who focus on others, not themselves. They ask questions of others. They listen and don't try to be the center of attention and they never try to pretend they're perfect.

- ✓ *A Servant Leader is Open to Learning From Others:* If you have ever met someone who felt compelled to play the expert all the time you will agree that such people aren't much fun to be around after a while, because the only input they seem open to is their own. And as the saying goes, people won't go along with you unless they can get along with you.

President Abraham Lincoln put it this way; he handled a person who had a know-it-all attitude.

Lincoln asked, "*How many legs will a sheep have if you call the tail a leg?*"

The man answered "*Five,*"

Lincoln replied "*No,*", "*he'll still have four, and because calling a tail a leg doesn't make it one.*"

Servant leaders are honest about their weaknesses and admit their faults to the people they work with. The people who work alongside you know your weaknesses, faults, and blind spots. If you doubt that and you have great courage just ask them! When you get real and admit your shortcomings. If you really desire others to see you as an approachable person, go a step beyond just willingness to admit your weaknesses.

Be willing to learn from them, each person we meet has the potential to teach us something, even though they are your subordinates don't shut them up and let them also know you are learning from them so that they will be free around you. Moses was open to receiving the help of other in his self-development. Moses' attitude teaches how to be a leader in hard times.

- ✓ *A Servant Leader Lead People So That they All Win Together*: Great leaders don't use people so that they can win. If that is truly your motivation, you can become the kind of person others want to follow whether they are beside, above or below you in the organizational hierarchy. The wonderful thing about helping others succeed is that it earns you more opportunities to help an even greater number of people. When you go out of your way to add value to your peers, they understand that you really want them to win with no hidden agenda of your own and this will increase their loyalty level because they feel a sense of pride and ownership.

- ✓ A servant leader needs to create the environment of respect and loyalty. Leaders must go further by placing a high premium on building loyalty. This is something that must be pursued on a daily basis. It calls for consistency. When people see broken promises, gossiping, withholding of information and when they feel that others have been placed high above them in spite of their commitment, their loyalty begins to wane.

Agile leaders don't vent about someone to others to make themselves feel better. If they have a problem with a person, they go to that individual and address the issue directly never through a third party. They raise publicly and criticize privately. And they never say anything about others that they wouldn't want them to hear because they probably will.

- ✓ A Servant Leader will emulate his principal leader with idealized influence. It is truth that behavior is learned not only by conditioning but by imitating persons with whom the learner identifies and whom he takes as models. Role modeling is yet another component of transformational leaders and has been referred to as idealized influence in particular leadership theory. As a transformational leader's follower you should emulate your leader with idealized influence because you can identify with them. Example the Pharisees couldn't differentiate Christ amongst his disciples.

Other contemporary leaders like Bishop David Oyedepo and Pastor David Abioye.

In another hand, followers also appreciate that the leaders have very high standards of moral, integrity and ethical conduct and can be counted on to do the right thing. Paul is quoted in ***1 Corin. 11:1-2' Be ye followers of me, even as I also am of Christ. Now I praise you, brethren, that ye remember me in all things, and keep the ordinances, as I delivered them to you.*** Another version renders is as try to imitate me, even as I myself try to imitate the Messiah. Timothy practically emulates Paul with idealized influence.

Nehemiah became a role mode to his people. By being the role model, he became the type of leader who "understands the way, follows the way, and shows his followers the way" A Servant Leader will expose his/her subordinates to good leadership resources and follow up the team to constantly improve and develop their capacity by encouraging them to listen to pastor's audio messages, read ministry books and attend trainings, praying for them as for the Lord rather than for men. ***Col. 3:23 "do it heartily, as to the Lord, and not to men"***

- ✓ Servant leaders act through a particular mindset, skills, and knowledge that emphasize involving others in decision-making. This model has a strong base in ethical and caring behavior. This create the kind of environment and the support system wherein spirited individuals can function

Typically, Nehemiah provided a positive role model for the postexilic people of Jerusalem and Judah. As governor, he was rewarded with a governor's allowance. He did not hoard material goods for himself; rather, he shared with the many poor around him. He provided them with food, as they had difficulty providing for their families. As Neh. 5:17-18 explained:

He protected his people from physical harm (Neh. 4:10) and from those who intend to cheat them (Neh. 5:8-9). He held fast to the Torah of God. His work ethic was strong as well. He easily could have delegated all work to his followers and subordinates, yet he labored at the task alongside them (Neh. 5:16).

- ✓ A servant leader fosters the context for agility by connecting teams with the organization's vision. To achieve that, Agile servant leaders facilitate communication around goals and coach teams to become autonomous and cross-functional. As a result, they improve effectiveness, enable organizations to adapt and evolve, and produce the expected results.

- ✓ A Servant Leader knows how crucial transparency, regular and direct communication is to success and actively creates an atmosphere for this. He promotes a collaborative approach within the team and attaches great importance to a functioning cooperation corporate culture. He is compassionate, shows sensitivity and emotional intelligence to empathize within the organization and always has an open ear for the team instead of exercising power and relying on rights that arise from a hierarchy.

- ✓ A Servant Leader Trust His Followers and their Skills. He is that one who really trusts the team members to make their own decisions, something that is extremely difficult for leaders with traditional leadership styles because they have never learned to give up control.

- ✓ A Servant Leader is modest by nature, takes himself back and supports the team members so that they can feel secure. This not only ensures that employees have the courage to bring out the best in themselves and to contribute their own ideas and solutions. It also makes sure that they trust you as a Servant Leader and follow you willingly and voluntarily.

- ✓ A Servant Leader maintains equanimity and integrity in crucial moments of decision making and during the intense periods of inherent chaos and uncertainty.

  Nehemiah averted a looming crisis by not paying attention to his external threats. He was steadfast when disgruntled Jews complained of their fellow Jews charging them interest (Neh. 5:1-13). When further opposition came from Sanballat and Geshem plotting against him, he pursued onward with the task at hand, not allowing them to veer him off his focus. The same held true when prophets like Noadiah attempted to intimidate him.

  Satan is greatly fighting for the church to get weaker, degenerate and die. Like Nehemiah, you persist even when adversity came. God's people cannot give up when adversity comes the Bible says in ***Proverbs***

24:10 "If thou faint in the day of adversity, thy strength is small" Nehemiah attention to his work and people never failed (Neh. 6:1-14). The perseverance paid off as the wall was complete. His vision became reality.

- ✓ A Servant Leader builds a sense of community across the organization. They encourage people to show sensitivity, compassion, and emotional intelligence to empathize within the organization

- ✓ A Servant Leader thinks and acts strategically, he/she creates a kind of safe and empowering environment where people can create; be productive, and where growths flourish. He facilitates and empowers people to make required decisions and enables the team to tap into its highest potential.

- ✓ A servant leader shows unconditional commitment to serving others' needs first instead of pursuing their own self-interest and ambitions. They actively listen to people's needs and wishes and align them with the organizational goals.

The best way to lead those that are positionally ahead of you is to let your own life be an example. Be willing to do what others are not doing; be available when there is a need. Loyalty pays, lead create and innovate give it quality mind attention.

CHAPTER SEVEN

==========================

THE CHALLENGES OF GRACE LEADERSHIP METHOD AND HOW TO CURB THEM

The Challenge when you are not a principal leader

Most declining churches grapple with weak and poor leadership. The crisis of weak, powerless, visionless, self-appointed and haughty leadership have done much havoc to the churches and followers end up being discourage because of the lack of progress and when discouragement and dissatisfaction sets in, it is very hard to enjoy the work.

When you are not a principal leader, which means you are not at the top position, you are just somewhere, you face lots of challenges that can frustrate you. As an agilist, you need to know that you will face them and be ready to conquer ***Rom 8:37 "Nay, in all these things we are more than conquerors through him that loved us."*** *Following are various challenges you might meet on your way if you are not the principal leader;*

I. You are going to face tension, you know the position of management and the reality on ground, you also understand the position of those at the bottom and the reality on ground causing you to be stocked in the middle to a point you are caught in-between.

II. The challenge of following an insecure and ineffective leader can also frustrate someone with a great zeal. People who follow income-petent Leaders often feel the pressure. Incompetent leaders are ineffective, and they often stay that way. They are trouble, not only for the people they lead, but also for their entire organization. You ask yourself don't pastor see, how did such a person become a coordinator you sit frustrated because you can't fight authority, you can't overthrow them, you can't rebel. But Grace Leadership approach tells us that even those that are at the top need to be led. So kingdom glory is not about self but you doing the righteousness of God.

III. The challenge that you will do the work but no one will credit you. Not everyone has the team spirit. Some are egotistical and feel all the accolades go to the one ahead of them. The greater your desire to receive credit and recognition, the more frustrated you are likely to become. This made you to contemplate why you should even do it while the pastor, HOD, CEO etc attention is on a particular person. You think you are working and someone else is taking your glory. Don't accept the adversary's suggestion, it is not about who is taking your glory, God sees your heart and will uplift you in his appointed time. True leadership is not being egotistical or wanting to be in the front. It is going ahead of others and being the first to get things done.

IV. The best way to lead those that are positionally ahead of you is to let your own life be an example. Be willing to do what others are not doing; be available when there is a need. Loyalty pays, lead create and innovate give it quality mind attention.

V. Another Grace Leadership approach challenge is that some thinks that can be fulfill only when they are at the top position and for people that can't really manage such desire, it will result to rebellion and scheming. You start looking for opportunity to pull down your fellow brethren. Winning at all costs will cost you when it comes to your peers. If your goal is to beat your peers, then you will never be that Grace/Agile leader. When you help the team, you're helping your leaders. And that gives the reasons to notice and appreciate you.

VI. The challenge of dealing with difficult people: You will meet different people at all levels but if you pick offence in their weakness, you will miss it. No matter how difficult an individual is, if you study them very well, you will know how to maintain and manage relationship. Understand that everyone have their strengths and weaknesses. Running away from problems is not the best way to handle that problem, you will not separate or abandoned your father or Mother because they are difficult, but you accommodate them. Likewise, focus on the strengths of those with you and the Lord will build you through them. The reason some pick offence and behave the way they behave is because they still have options but if you will looked at it as they were your parents, husband, wife or children, you will never leave them because they are difficult.

Additionally, before you decide to leave the Church because the pastor, pastors wife, HOD, leader etc is difficult, have a second though, there are difficult members but a pastor will never leave Church because you are difficult. Look at things from the point of destiny and not of convenience because of the part it is playing in your destiny. If worst comes to worst, as a child of God you pray for God to intervene, or for the grace to handle it and development to grow to handle and accommodate all kinds of people. Built that immunity through prayer, if not you will be fighting a battle without the spoil and that is not an achievement.

However, if you find yourself in a situation where you are considering leaving an organization, make sure you're not doing it because of selfishness or ego. Fight that urge. It is unwelcoming to leave the church based on flimsy and humane mistake. Learn to work with your leader's weakness. If you make your leader your adversary, you will create a no-win situation. Instead, build a relational bridge. It is better to find a way to succeed with people who are hard to work with. Why do you do it? Because it benefits you and the organization, how do you do it? Try to get to know him/her, find common ground, connect with them and build a solid relationship. And instead of putting these difficult people in your place, you try to put yourself in their place. And in that process, reaffirm your commitment to the mission of the organization. Sales expert and author Les Giblin said, "*You can't make the other fellow feel important in your presence if you secretly feel that he is a nobody.*" Likewise, you can't build a positive relationship with your boss if you secretly disrespect him because of his weaknesses.

Since everybody has blind spots and weak areas, why not learn to work with them? Everybody has strengths even an ineffective leader. Work to find them in the person you work for. Maybe it won't be easy. Maybe his strengths aren't qualities you value or admire. That doesn't matter. Find them, and then think about how they might be assets to the organization. Try to focus on the positives, and work around the negatives. To do anything else will only hurt you.

VII. The *challenge of Personality Management*: Know when to push, and when to back off. You need to realize that the stronger your natural desire to initiate, the greater the potential for tension. If you continually push the limits, it's likely you will rub others the wrong way. In order to make this better, understand the person you are relating with because every relationship have it boundaries and if you cross them, you will begin to cause issues that could have possibly been avoided. Let your suggestion be like a suggestion and not a command. So don't impose your idea in such a way that if it is not taken, it becomes a problem. However, become that person that everyone will be happy to associate with. Be that good team player that everyone will desire you to be in their team. Get better day by day and make yourself valuable by giving your leader unique and vital information.

In a nut shell I encourage you to learn to lead despite the restrictions others have placed on you. If you are a not the principal leader, I will tell you, you have a challenging task. You might likely be frustrated, tense and even tempted to quite. Thing like this will pop up your mind, No matter how hard I try, I never seem to get anywhere." "I really wonder if it's all worth it." Perhaps you feel you have been struggling to succeed where you are. Nevertheless, Patience, determination and responsibility will take you there.

The Challenge when you are the principal Leader

Everything rises and falls on leadership so say John Maxwell. The leadership that feels threatened by the success and achievements of others will remain lonely and forsaken and the church will be greatly impaired. If they don't have a united heart with the leaders all efforts will be futile. Only autocratic Leadership hates suggestions, contributions, advice and inputs.

Nehemiah gained the trust of the people. This permitted him to build a team that could make the vision happen. People shared responsibility to accomplish the goal. No one person, not even Nehemiah, could accomplish this vision alone. The talents of the people were named and used (***chapter 3***). Different people worked on different sections of the wall. People were assigned to work closest to their homes. Take football team sport, for instance, it involves eleven individuals in the pitch, each with a specific role to play yet collaboration is the key to victory especially number nine and ten have to collaborate no matter how selfish they are. The energy, focus and collaboration of each is combined to produce the outcome. Our desire is to work as one body. God give us the grace to esteem other better than ourselves, to collaborate, appreciate one another in Unity. Therefore, the leader and its subordinate must present a united front; there must be unity of purpose. Every hand must be on deck. Everybody must play his/ her part very well. Following are some challenges encounted by principal leaders;

I. The problem for many leaders is that they end up competing against their peers in their own organization in a way that hurts the team and them. When it comes to your teammates, try much in such a way that instead of competing with them, you complete them.

   Team work creates synergy, when people are united they stand together and everyone brings something to the table. Team work allows those who are specialist to focus on their area of strength and this helps to cover the blind side. With this, it helps us to get the perspective we have never possessed, but is in other people. The strength of individual increases as the leaders masters the people capabilities and limitations and also keeps the team members informed and develop a sense of responsibility with them.

II. The Challenge of Insecure Leaders in the Church. A typical example is King Saul; he was an insecure leader who even wishes the death of his servant David. Due to insecurity, a whole king left the throne in search of the young David in the cave, what a horrible mistake.

Insecure leaders think everything is about them, and as a result, every action, every piece of information, every decision is put through their filter of self-centeredness. When someone on their team performs exceptionally well, they fear being outshone, and they often try to keep him from rising up. When someone on their team does poorly, they react in anger because it makes them look bad. This attitude is destructive and you must fight it out of you.

In order to kill such spirit, I advise you shouldn't keep your best stuff to yourself. Our natural tendency is to protect what's ours, whether it's our turf, our ideas, or our resources. But if you share what you have when it can help others, you really send a positive message to the people who work with you. So don't be afraid to create the right environment from which great oak trees will emerge; feed them with the right materials, the right meetings, the right method of challenging and mentoring; and by helping them to hone their leadership skills, reduce workload, increases productivity and reduces stress.

As the saying goes, when you light another's candle, you lose nothing of your own. You just produce more light. Contribute to the progress of those at the same level with you and around you. Remove the mindset that when you contribute to their progress, part of yours will be cutoff and your value be diminished, the sky is big enough for everyone to fly without hitting one another. When you contribute in the life of people, they will never forget you. Success is when all the people around you are doing, well. Built relationships with the people you desire to lead. You treat them with dignity and respect. Value them as human beings and care about them, not just the job they can do for you.

III. The challenge of Vision Casting: The vision must be strategic and well communicated to the team, get their bargain so that when the vision is being shared, it will be "*It is our vision*" because people find it difficult to follow a vision they did not initiate. Vision powers the mission, motivates and helps people to know where they are going, identify the challenges ahead and to proffer the necessary solutions. God told Moses to tell the people, you are going to a land that is flowing with milk and honey, a land with grounds good for agriculture. So the leader would serve the vision broadly and deeply enough to inspire other people to want to participate.

Also, Nehemiah didn't merely state the vision to King Artaxerxes, but to the people of Jerusalem, of whom he garnered support and used his closeness to King Artaxerxes to his advantage and receive help. Three days after arriving in Jerusalem, he said, *"You see the trouble we are in: Jerusalem lies in ruins, and its gates have been burned with fire. Come, let us rebuild the wall of Jerusalem, and we will no longer be in disgrace" (Nehemiah 2:17).*

He assured them that God graced him with the plan and the king backed him. Their response to Nehemiah's vision was well received, that God has answered their prayers as the people happily proclaimed ***"Let us arise and start rebuilding," (Nehemiah 2:18-20).*** **The people needed to hear Nehemiah's vision, Proverbs *29:18 says it all, "Where there is no vision, the people perish."* Nehemiah successfully pointed the people toward the planned future goal, energized people and commitment, gave them the reason to work, and established a standard of excellence.**

Even when God's, people were tired. They felt the task was taking too much time and was too difficult, still Nehemiah was able to find ways to alleviate their concerns without losing the vision.

Be clear with the vision and the objective and role people are to play and stand by them as they go through the process by empowering them to speak their mind, express what motivates them and by giving them a certain degree of authority. This will demonstrate that you trust them and by so doing, the leader will be freed to find new horizons.

IV. The challenge of dealing with Confrontations: Most spiritual leaders will face opposition in trying to accomplish the will of God. These leaders have to "welcome conflict as a heart-shaping tool of God" In doing so, he proved himself an exemplary leader; John Maxwell *said "A true test of great leadership is the ability to recognize a problem before it becomes an emergency".* Let the truth be told, a successful leader will have to deal with confrontation on a daily basis. Either his actions will provoke it, or his desire to bring a change will make it happen. Some confrontations are necessary; nevertheless separate the person from the behavior. Never attack the person, don't let the personality of someone you work with cause you to lose sight of the greater purpose, which is to add value to the team and advance the organization. If that means listening to the ideas of people with whom you have no chemistry, or worse, a difficult history, so be it. The leadership that is unforgiving and rigid will always lose quality and God sent workers and helpers.

More so, when dealing with confrontation as a leader, it is important that you are compass-ionate and realize that at the end of the day the dignity and value of the person must not be torn to shreds just because we are dealing with them. Avoid pride, listen to them and in cases where you must reject the ideas of others, make sure you reject only the idea and not the Person. However, be genuine in your responses but never condescend. Rather, take your stand and never behave as if you are superior to the person whose issues you are dealing with. ***Ecclesiastes 4:9 (NKJV) "Two are better than one, because they have a good reward for their labor."***

Deuteronomy 32:30 (NKJV) "How could one chase a thousand, And two put ten thousand to flight, unless their Rock had sold them, and the Lord had surrendered them?"

Nevertheless, God's leader is not discouraged by adversity. Nehemiah was ready for the conflict and for the work to be accomplished; he developed a protective plan to station guards at the points of highest risk, dividing the workforce into guards and construction workers. He also appointed people who watched day and night against their enemies. ***Nehemiah 4:16-18 And it came to pass from that time forth, that the half of my servants wrought in the work, and the other half of them held both the spears, the shields, and the bows, and the habergeons; and the rulers were behind all the house of Judah. They which builded on the wall, and they that bare burdens, with those that laded, every one with one of his hands wrought in the work, and with the other hand held a weapon. For the builders, every one had his sword girded by his side, and so builded. And he that sounded the trumpet was by me.***

V. The challenge of fear and apathy: A leader can be discouraged or dissatisfied if those who should praise and appreciate him with whole recognition and reward do the opposite, or do nothing. To overcome self-doubt, disillusionment and discouragement the leader must learn to create positive actions while standing against the flow of discouragement. When the leader is an example people will be committed to see the vision happen. ***"For God has not given us a spirit of timidity, but of power and love and discipline" (2 Tim. 1:7)***

VI. The Challenge of Lazy and unfaithful *Leaders:* Leaders must be ready to work very hard and must not be a lazy, indolent and prayerless person. He must buckle up and get down to serious and hard work and "take risk" risk taking is one element of success that we cannot ignore any longer. Taking calculated risk is the sure mark of great leadership and no leader can record any worthwhile achievement without risk taking. Leadership that is afraid of taking risks cannot lead people up but down. The ability to take risk is one attribute that pastors of mega churches possess in abundance.

VII. The challenges of rejection from people as leader can also be discouraged or disillusioned, if all he hears is criticism from the side lines, or receives an attitude from people that suggests they know better than he does.

Mark it that those who make up their mind to make a difference do not internalize every negative feedback they get. Neither do they sit down only to count the mistakes and negative comments leveled at them. Also recognize the fact that attitude is everything. If you have only a negative attitude, it will eat up your self-esteem and create an atmosphere of self-doubt.

Develop a strong personality, strong personality leader are always at the top. They are not afraid of what others will say or do, if not, they cannot do a lasting work for God. If they are always swayed by people opinions and are willing to bow down to the selfish interest of antagonists in the name of peace, they cannot make any serious impact for God. Great leaders are men who can take the bull by the horn and march on for God, regardless of negative comments and opposition of envious people. However, surrounding yourself with a degree of positive affirmation from the people who value what you are doing is advisable.

VIII. The challenge of celebrating victories: When people work so hard to accomplish a great goal, the temptation is to want to stop and rest. God's people should stop and celebrate victories. The leader must realize that it is important to celebrate achievement. Celebration is good because people become battle weary if there is nothing to celebrate. Everyone gets excited about the vision and the set goals. However, once it is achieved there is rarely ever an acknowledgement of the employees who made it happen. This can sometimes result in a loss of motivation and a lack of desire to work as hard as they did on the previous project. The celebration of victory is a valuable opportunity to send a message to the workers that they are valued, appreciated and that they are the ones who have made the achievements of the organization happen.

IX. The Challenge of Followers with constant feeling of dissatisfaction: Identify with their challenges, discouragements and disappointments. People find it easy to follows a leader who knows how to identify with the things they are going through. A good leader uses a persuasive and not commanding approach. He will use democracy as a good tool for challenging others to run with him and not a demon that reduces his power.

X. The Challenge of Managing Scandal: Avoid scandals and impropriety, scandals and impropriety give the church a bad image in the community which in-turn will definitely affect the health of the church. Crisis, chaos, moral lapses and financial misdeeds paint the church in bad image to the people. Many get this out of order, and weak character sabotages their success, the people remain unconvinced about the sincerity and genuineness of the church as a result of these unfortunate scenarios. A leader must realize he'll answer to God for everything, work, relationships, and lifestyle.

XI. The leader must be a person of Integrity and remain a faithful steward. A "doer of the Word," by applying God's principles to every decision and realize the importance of pursuing holiness and practicing self- discipline and doing the right thing, whether or not he feels like it. Many over-simplify integrity and miss the extreme importance of this quality. Living by faith and being trustworthy are the main components of faithfulness.

That means seeking and trusting God in pursuing the mission He's given us with courage, taking risks, and persevering in hope through difficult times. We are called to rest on His character, rely on His promises, and do things in His way, not ours. Integrity is multidimensional and in order to achieve integrity, you must be completely aligned with the will of God, courageously exercises self-discipline, daily indwelling of the person of the Holy Spirit before they can focus on leading others.

XII. The Challenge of Internal Politics and lack of Honesty: There is this internal politics to contend with. Polluted atmosphere as a result of bickering will always work against the well-being of the church, holy alliances that borders on class, tribe and self cannot augur well for the church. It is sad when decisions have political undertone. The leader must aspire and motivate the people to work together as a team for maximum results. There must be no favoritism and respect of persons. Sacred cows, untouchable and preferential treatments must never be allowed to ruin the harmony that is greatly needed for achievements.

XIII. Additionally, the leader must be honest, either it is or it is not, either it's black or white. **Truth, define the reality of the situation. Peter Senge said "Unless the reality can be described honestly, progress is impossible. "Nothing is more limiting to a group, than the inability to talk about the truth."**

"In a time of universal deceit, telling the truth becomes a revolutionary act." George Orwell

Today, we hide our dishonesty behind such euphemisms as 'gray areas,' 'half-truths,' or 'little white lies. The truth is that honesty begins with us. Dishonesty is usually easy to spot and powerfully detrimental to an organization. So, for the leader to be an example of Christ to non-believing and believing members, honesty is extremely important. Without complete honesty, trust is lost and relationships suffer. Building team spirit means the leader must be adept in the act of encouraging others. By words, actions and inactions, he must be an encourager, thereby bringing the best from the people.

Above all, the leader is characterized by love. In Scripture, the word "love" is not only feeling based, but a deliberate decision. Jesus' Great Commandment is to love God and love people (**Mark 12:30-31**). The place must be given for the power of the Holy Spirit and prayers to direct the affairs of the church/

department. From that relationship, the fruit of the Spirit is manifest and his character becomes extra-ordinary as Holy Spirit is the workings that will bring growth and vitality to the church. Moses insisted on the leading and presence of God, otherwise he would not continue. Then he said to him, ***"if your presence does not go with us, don't bring us up from here". Exodus33:15***

The Challenge of Transitioning Leadership

"What you have heard from me in the presence of many witnesses entrust to faithful men who will be able to teach others also." **(2 Timothy 2:2).**

Some leaders may feel like something is being given away. No matter how much people express their humility, they may not realize how easily their ego can come in and starve the organization of its chance to develop other talents for the future. Leadership success makes the leader attractive to a certain number of people. However, his chances of influencing the people he needs to raise for the future may reduce. These reasons given, and many more, highlight the challenges of raising future leaders because not every leader empowers as they should.

If you are a leader, a pastor or an elder, and you are not influencing anyone, you are not leaving any legacy. Your leadership success is when you build future leaders. Men do build a legacy for their children what of a spiritual legacy, made up of spiritual children who can take after you, those that will reflect your leadership qualities. An empowering leader develops a strategy that has raising other leaders as one of its end goals.

Jesus prepared leaders to take after Him, ***Mark 3:13-14 "And he went up on the mountain and called to him those whom he desired, and they came to him. And he appointed twelve…so that they might be with him and he might send them out to preach."***

Apostle Paul did same: ***Acts 20:27 "For I did not shrink from declaring to you the whole counsel of God."***

Paul passed the baton to Timothy to do same: ***Acts 20:27 "What you have heard from me in the presence of many witnesses entrust to faithful men who will be able to teach others also."***

As a servant Leader, you are called to do same.

Levels of authority are a necessity because they give people positions to aspire to. The Bible does not speak against a good, honest aspiration to lead, and be in front.

CHAPTER EIGHT

=====================

THE NEW TESTAMENT WAY OF SELECTING AND PROMOTING A LEADER TO THE NEXT LEVEL

Introduction

The Desire for Leadership must be motivated by the Holy Spirit "***Be on guard for yourselves and for all the flock, among which the Holy Spirit has made you overseers, to shepherd the church of God." (Acts 20:28)***

1 Timothy 3-7 gives us a vivid bible standard of the New Testament way of selecting a leader. ***"[It is] certain, if anyone is desirous of the episcopal office, he desireth a good work. A bishop then must be blameless, the husband of [but] one wife, sober, prudent, grave, hospitable, able to teach, not given to wine, no striker, not greedy of sordid gain, moderate, not quarrelsome, not covetous, governing his own family well, having his children in subjection with all gravity; (for if any [one] know not how to govern his own house, how shall he take care of the church of God?) not one newly converted, least being puffed up he fall into the condemnation of the devil. He ought***

also to have an honorable testimony from those that are without, least he fall into reproach and the snare of the devil".

2 Timothy 2:2-4 "and [the things] which thou hast heard from me, before many witnesses, these commit to faithful men, who shall be able to teach others also. Do thou therefore endure hardship, as [becomes] a good soldier of Jesus Christ. No one that enters into military service embarrasseth himself with the affairs of [this] life, that he may please him who enlisted [him.]"

The New Testament way of selecting a leader that Paul was prescribing to the church and specifically to Timothy could also be related with the corporate world. In the corporate world, we work for different organizations and when employed, there are terms and conditions of service that makes you work in line with the job's prescription.

Positional power makes the job so much easier to move things through the organization and get things done. However, a leader must understand that if he value and treats people fairly, they will not only achieve more; jobs will be completed faster and better and changes will be implemented more easily. People who are committed to the vision must be treated fairly.

Levels of authority are a necessity because they give people positions to aspire to. The Bible does not speak against a good, honest aspiration to lead, and be in front. Rather, it teaches us to desire the office but totally opposes illicit desire for position, particularly when it is for personal aggrandizement. Nevertheless, the delegation of control and authority may either be done according to the level of the person's maturity or the willingness of the leader who delegates.

Things to consider while choosing or promoting a Leader to a top position

1. The person's last level of obedience, or allegiance to the organization/company's goal, vision, policy and leadership should be thoroughly examined. Rebellion and act of insubordination must be crushed and not condone.

2. Take into consideration the team the person will work with, if it is good for the company because some individuals have a high intelligence quotient but very low emotional intelligence or an ability to connect with people on an emotional level.

3. It should be consider if the person has a team approach to making decisions, making sure you are not promoting an autocrat.

4. Don't overlook the amount of respect they command from the other team members, make an evaluation.

Evaluate whether this leader in the making is dedicated to the course, purpose or vision of the organization. Do they see the overall mission and goal of the church as something that they embrace and are ready to serve? The leader in the making must also be matured enough so that the promotion does not make them haughty.

Potential leaders adapt well to change and opposition. By listening to his people, Nehemiah stayed abreast of changes and adapted readily and effectively. When apprised of the external threats from enemies, such as Sanballat, Geshem and Tobiah, Nehemiah first prayed, as was typically his first line of defense against adversaries. Despite the opposition from adversaries, Nehemiah persevered. In fact, he showed tenacity throughout the entire project. For example, Nehemiah could have easily listened to his brother Hanani explain about the distress of the Jews and, while wanting to do something about it, convince himself that he did not have the opportunity to accomplish the task of rebuilding since he already had a responsibility as cupbearer to Artaxerxes. Instead, he persevered with the vision of the reconstruction by requesting a leave of absence from his duties.

Joshua sat at the foot of the mountain waiting for Moses during period he went to the top of the mountain for 40 days. It is important that when a person is committed to leadership, that he is unafraid to work hard or put in the extra hours when needed. He/she shouldn't be like Mark in the evangelical team of Apostle Paul (*It is recorded that when the heats were on, Mark couldn't endure, so he left and abandoned Apostle Paul and Barnabas in Pamphylia, they were left alone to face the persecution,*) Acts 13:4 ***Acts 15:37-9 "And Barnabas determined to take with them John, whose surname was Mark. But Paul thought not good to take him with them, who departed from them from Pamphylia, and went not with them to the work. And the contention was so sharp between them, that they departed asunder one from the other..."*** Apostle Paul was keen enough to observe such attitude from Mark, that his loyalty was not complete, as a result he disagreed strongly to take Mark for their second missionary journey, Paul does needed a strong partner who can withstand spiritual and physical persecution. Eventually Paul found Silas who will be with him in the prison in Phillippi.

2 Samuel 1:11 ***"Then David took hold on his clothes, and rent them; and likewise all the men that were with him"*** that shows loyalty.

While many stop trying to reach a goal when troubles arise, those who persevere continue on in order to "see a commitment through to completion. Taunting enemies failed to slow Nehemiah's work. Even though they threatened to send a report back to Artaxerxes that Nehemiah was fomenting a rebellion. Nehemiah replied in effect, We will continue our work.' Nehemiah gave them a remarkable answer: ***I am doing a great work, so that I cannot come down: why should the work cease?' (Neh. 6:3.)***

Like John Mark in Pamphylia, too many of us are ready on the slightest suggestion to give up the important work that we are doing. What a lesson Nehemiah teaches us! Ridicule, fear, threats, union of forces and organization against him, and an offer to compromise, all failed to move him, or to delay the thing he had set his hand to do a single day."

Additionally, if anything, leadership quality is better demonstrated when you find a person who not only has the ability to perform the task, but also possess the extra ability to raise future leaders as well.

5. A leader, who is due for promotion, must show the ability to manage time and delegate jobs to other members of the team. If there is any litmus test for this person, it must be their

ability to easily transition from being a regular team member, to a team leader without victimizing those they lead.

If the person is unable to lead comfortably without sacking everyone around them, then they may not be qualified for such elevation. It has been known for a person to be elevated to the position of team leader and they immediately either relegate their fellow team members or ask them to leave.

Promoting people from within the system is a great solution to vacancies, particularly, if there is someone or people who have shown leadership potential. However, guard against promoting people for the wrong reasons, i.e. because they suck up to the leader and flatter those in authority or who have been in the organization for a long time. Immature leadership accounts for many decisions that have hurt the very people whom the leader purports to represent. When the leadership is immature, responsibility and decision making is shallow and based on the mundane. These are not good reasons for putting them in a position of leadership.

Eradicate the mindset that it is when you get to the top that you will beat all limitations.

Chapter Nine

Destroying the Sacred Cows of Leadership

We are called to exude the glory of God everywhere we go and one of the ways is in leadership. Others believe that only the pastor that is a leader. To be Christ ambassador, you must be a leader from your domain of operation even if you are not the principal leader. Even an average individual, still process leadership skills, your leadership potential can be developed if you are willing to work at it. Following are some leadership myths that have been upheld, which limits many from exercising their leadership capacity.

- **The Believe That Effective leadership is by the top position:** The truth is that, for you to be a leader, you don't need to be at the top. You don't have to be that "*perfect person*" or believe that you are not good enough and that leadership is given to a certain caliber of people. If you are willing to enhance your God given potentials you will be amazed of what you carry. You don't necessarily need a position to be a leader, understand that you can effectively lead, even if you are not at the top. For example, you might be a PhD holder and when it comes to mending your shoe or dress, you go to either a shoe mender or a fashion designer; invariably they become your leaders in their domain. Many, especial children of God bury their potentials and limit what they can do in the house of God because they are not in any position. Don't wait for position or titles to lead; it is your heart that justifies you before God, not your position.

In a certain church, a sister had a vision that someone great in the church passed on and everyone thought it was the pastor. Ironically the vision was directed to an elderly woman in the church. She was a great intercessor; she will come early, and clean the chairs while interceding for the lives of those that will sit on them. This emphasizes that, effective leadership is not by position but by performance. A lot of things are still left undone in the house of God because as a believer, you have not taken responsibility to stand as a representation of the kingdom. You might see the needs but not fill in because you expect someone else to do. As long as you have the Holy Spirit in you, you are a potential leader in the house of God.

A typical example is the Samaritan woman in the **John 4**, she had five failed marriages yet Jesus Christ chose her. He needed her to go to the city and proclaim the Gospel. She ran to the city to herald the presence of the messiah amongst them. Before Philip ever went to Samaria to preach the Gospel, the Samaritan woman has watered the ground long before he came. ***1Cor 1:26-27 "For ye see [by] your calling, brethren, that not many wise [men] according to the flesh, not many mighty, not many noble [are called:] but God hath chosen [things that are] foolish [in the eye] of the world to put [it's] wise men to confusion; and God hath chosen the weak [things] of the world to confound the mighty;"*** Meaning, your family background, your past and what you've gone through in life doesn't matter. Whatever you have to offer your local Church assembly, society or company the moment you begin to do it, you are pathing your way to the top.

- ***The thought that only those that find their way to top can effectively lead.*** You must not get to the top before you learn to lead. Our God is a God of time and chances, What if circumstances catapults you to the top, is it then that you will begin to learn how to lead? You would be deceiving yourself, if you think that till you get to the top that is when you will learn to lead, you will not succeed because you cannot be learning to lead, when you are supposed to be leading. You are trying to get the weapons of war on the battlefield. Some of you have this mentality; they will say it is pastor's, HOD, etc. responsibility. David started leading his father's sheep and from the shepherd boy to the killing of Goliath, good leadership is learned in the trenches. Leading as well as they can wherever they are is what prepares leaders for more and greater responsibility. Becoming a good leader is a lifelong learning process. If you don't try out your leadership skills and decision-making process when the stakes are small and the risks are low, you're likely to get into trouble at higher levels when the cost of mistakes is high, the impact is far reaching, and the exposure is greater. Mistakes made on a small scale can be easily overcome while mistakes made when you're at the top cost the organization greatly, and can damage a leader's credibility.

Therefore, Whatever idea you have now, start implementing it without delay, that is what makes you a solution provider, that will path the way to leadership, the Bible says a man's gift makes way for him, your gift, your idea and councils will make way for you. Am certain that the life of the slave girl after giving the solution for Naaman sickness would never have been the same, it would have brought a positive impact on her life.

- ***Get rid of the mindset that people will not adhere unless you are at top.*** That is why we talk of us to esteem one another above ourselves, I will not despise your council just because am the pastor, HOD or deacon and you are not. You on the other side should not feel intimidated by position. When your light is shining whether you are at the top or not people follow you. A case in point is Moses in Egypt, God called and sent him to Pharaoh and backed him up with divine ability to carry out the unprecedented mandate. Brethren bear in mind that, the Calling is your authority; it is not your certificates, your background nor your good command of English language. People don't just follow people, people follow visions and results.

John Wesley once said *"Light yourself on fire with passion and people will come from miles to watch you burn."* After the death of his father, Wesley was forbidden to preach inside the church at Epworth; thus, he used his father's tombstone in the churchyard as a pulpit. Wesley later wrote *"I found such a congregation as I believe Epworth never saw before...I stood near the east end of the church, upon my father's tomb stone and cried"*, ***"The kingdom of heaven is not meat and drink, but righteousness, and peace, and joy in the Holy Ghost."***.

There are certain people you meet and you might not have followed them just for the sake of followership, it is the impact they brought in your life that made you follow them. You go to a particular church because of the impact and transformation the church is bringing to your life. For examples, to some I am their Pastor, to some I am their Counselor, some and their mentor, life coach and role model and to some I am simply Mr. Victor Mbah. Your mindset about me is transformed due to the impact I bring to your life. So it is wrong to think that people will not follow you, the fact that you have a place you are going is an assurance that people will adhere. The disciples of Jesus Christ all have gainful employment but left to follow Jesus Christ, what made them follow him is what he carried in him that was manifested in the outside. He spoke about his vision with boldness and assurance, which gave them confidence to follow him.

Another typical example is when David escaped King Saul's assassination and hide in the cave, the Bible says 400 men came to him, in distress, debt and discontented ***1Sam 22:1 "David therefore departed thence, and escaped to the cave Adullam: and when his brethren and all his father's house heard it, they went down thither to him. And every one that was in distress, and every one that was in debt, and***

every one that was discontented, gathered themselves unto him; and he became a captain over them: and there were with him about four hundred men." Though David didn't have the means to solve their problems but they saw in him the future solution for their problems, they saw a giant with a great vision inside the young David, though he was in the cave. The bible later says David transformed them to be mighty men of David a loyal army for David ***2Sam 23:8-39***. Some marvel at the level of our progress as a church, some wonder how someone like me who grew in Africa can have such mindset in leading **Omega Gospel Ministries** to this level but that is God at work in me. Those of you that are married, your wife saw your vision, your focus before accepting you, you might not have had any physical means to show but they saw greatness in you and followed destiny.

- ***Destroy the mentality that when you get to the top you will be in control***; You are already in control now even though you feel inexperience; God in you is doing the work. ***Philippians 2:13 "for it is God that worketh in you both to will, and to work, out of [his own] good-pleasure".*** It is the level of your output that determines your results, you are how you are because of the way you pilot your life.

I for one never knew I will be a Pastor, as I saw the church struggled for finance, my vision was to be an evangelist that will do business and sponsor the work of God, sponsor crusade. I saw the sufferings of humanity become so compassionate, that is how I began my calling as a pastor, and the Lord built my mentality toward it. He graced me in such a way that I don't struggle in it. The character just flow, God has fought my battles all the way.

Don't be too careful not to fail; failure is included in the pathway to success. It is better to make mistakes than to fake perfection. Mistakes are real, so your approach to it will make the difference, accepting, the consequences of failure is not a sign of weakness, but rather a measure of leadership. Nobody likes to fail. However, the acceptance of the failure will help a leader to move forward, the leader who shows courage forgets fear and sees results. "*Success is the result of perfection, hard work, learning from failure, loyalty and persistence.*" **Collin Powell.**

- ***Eradicate the mindset that it is when you get to the top that you will beat all limitations.*** Some of you take pretense that you are not at the top yet, you are not a pastor, or HOD or deacon yet, you are still under authority and that is why you can't do anything to change the situation. At whatever level you find yourself there are many things you can do. If you can do what you do effectively, freedom will be released. When you work efficiently with task delegated to you, you will also be appraised and given more opportunities.

Some think they can't reach their potentials if they are not at the top. That is the main reason you see some pastor break away to start their own ministry, they want to be the pastor, General overseer and the likes, but that is not how easy it is. There are many in pastoral works who are not called to be pastors and to an extent, they have polluted the minds of some people in such a way that they criticize even those that are genuinely called to ministry.

Take up the challenge and fulfill your part. I believe that people who consider the opinions of others too much often perform too little. You start now to adopt the thinking, learn the skills, and develop the habits of the person you wish to be. It's a mistake to daydream. Look at the need in the house of God and fit in, knowing that you will give an account to God and that will bring you the blessings.

In the same vein, destroy the mind that encourages you to complacently remain in your comfort zone. Some think there are being ignored and despised so they better remain in their position and don't just vent in matters that does not concerns them. The church of Jesus Christ it is not the pastor's property or a one man show. We all get involved.

The body of Christ is one make of many members like you and I. The body has different parts and we are all members of the same body, one cannot say he doesn't need other because we need each other to function smoothly. How do you feel when you stay away from church for a time and do come only when it is convenience for you or when you have an issue? You feel you are not accountable to anyone. What if everyone will behave in like manner? You can't do that in your secular job. We are given everyone the opportunity to express our God given gifts.

CHAPTER TEN

=============

Quick Test Of Effective Servant Leadership

We have explored all the aspects of servant leadership and how it can be a great force in enabling agile transformation in the organization. However, how would any organization or a servant leader know if the philosophy of Agile servant leadership has indeed yielded its expected results across the organization?

Following is a quick test of effective servant leadership:

1. If you are able to see and feel the growth of the people who are being served
2. If people are wiser, healthier, empowered, and more driven
3. If you are able to sense more harmony and more collaboration between the people
4. If people are inspired enough to perform the role of a servant leader themselves
5. Evaluate how your servant leadership affects the under-resourced segment of the church /community

If most of the results of the above are positive, congratulations! Your servant leadership has indeed served its true purpose. If most of them are negative, it only means your organization still has work left to do. Your servant leadership style needs some more time, patience, and practice so that the highest organizational and individual potential can be tapped into. And, where there is a will, there is always a way!

The End

==================================

For additional information about Omega Gospel Ministries, Email: omegahouston@yahoo.com

Visit our Website

https://www.omegagospelministries.com/Facebook page

https://www.facebook.com/OmegaGospelMinistries/
or write to these addresses

USA Address: Omega Gospel Ministries
11796 S. Glen Dr.
Houston, Texas 77099

==========================

Decision Page

I want to invite you to make Jesus your Lord and personal Savior if you have not done so. Boycott hell and embrace eternal life given through believing in Jesus as your Lord and personal Savior. Prayer and fasting will not work if you do not belong to the kingdom of God, and if you don't with sincerity of heart declare for Jesus. If today, you agree to give your life to Jesus, the sample prayer below will change your life and relationship for the better. God is the author of marriage, He will give you the best of it.

Please pray:
Dear Jesus, I believe you died for me and that you rose again on the third day. I confess to you that I am a sinner and that I need your love and forgiveness. Come into my life, forgive my sins, and turn my life around. With my mouth I confess that you are the son of God. In my heart I believe that God raised you from the dead. I declare that you are my Lord and Master. Thank You Jesus. From today, help me to walk in your peace, love, forgiveness and joy forever.

Signed: ______________________________________

Date: ______________________________________

Call for counseling or ministration
Contact me at: 832-887-7105

Notes

www.ingramcontent.com/pod-product-compliance
Lightning Source LLC
LaVergne TN
LVHW091326150826
845673LV00006B/1781

* 9 7 9 8 3 8 5 8 1 3 6 5 0 *